Comments on
the Oxford Research Group International Security Reports:

Incisive, elegant, profound: if you want to understand what happened and why, you should start here.

George Monbiot, journalist and commentator, *The Guardian*

Paul Rogers' reports are a must read for those who want to know the truth about the situation in Iraq. This collection of his writings tracks how we got into such a mess and the options for the future.

Clare Short, former Secretary of State for International Development

The clarity of the analysis in these monthly digests stands the test of time, unlike much daily journalism. Paul Rogers is a secular prophet for our troubled age. It should be required reading in the Pentagon. The fact that it won't be is part of the problem.

David Loyn, BBC

Paul Rogers has proved himself, time and again, to be a dispassionate analyst of events in Iraq and the wider 'war on terror'. Had his comments been taken on board by President Bush's advisers, the world might be a safer place; as it is, Rogers sees only hard times ahead. The war against al-Qaeda is not being won, and visions of American hegemony in the Persian Gulf, thanks to a client state in Iraq, are but a pipedream. This is hardly the dawn of the New American Century as imagined by its mentors in Washington: Rogers is a must-read for all politicians, the media and academics alike.

Tom Walker, *Sunday Times*

Oxford Research Group
International Security Report July 2005

Paul Rogers is Professor of Peace Studies at Bradford University and recently completed a two-year term as Chair of the British International Studies Association. He is widely quoted as a security expert and has published extensively on the subject.

The **Oxford Research Group** is the prestigious research and advocacy group working in the areas of human security and international cooperation, based in Oxford.
www.oxfordresearchgroup.org.uk

IRAQ

and the war on terror

Twelve months of insurgency 2004/2005

Paul Rogers

I.B. TAURIS

LONDON · NEW YORK

Published in 2006 by I.B.Tauris & Co Ltd
6 Salem Road, London W2 4BU
175 Fifth Avenue, New York NY 10010
www.ibtauris.com

In the United States of America and in Canada distributed by
Palgrave Macmillan, a division of St Martin's Press
175 Fifth Avenue, New York NY 10010

ISBN 1 84511 205 9
EAN 978 184511 205 9

A full CIP record for this book is available from the British Library
A full CIP record for this book is available from the Library of
Congress

Library of Congress catalog card: available

Typeset in Palatino Linotype by Steve Tribe, Andover
Printed and bound in Great Britain by MPG Books Ltd, Bodmin

Contents

Acknowledgements

I would like to thank the Director of the Oxford Research Group, Professor John Sloboda, and members of staff, especially Chris Abbott, James Kemp and Rosie Holdsworth, for assistance and ideas in the production of this report.

I would also like to thank Dr Scilla Elworthy, who originally proposed the idea of a series of monthly briefings, and Gabrielle Rifkind for hosting a number of discussions relating to Iraq and the war on terror.

Introduction

A fter the attacks in New York and Washington on 11 September 2001, the Oxford Research Group published a number of studies concerning the developing 'global war on terror'. These included wide-ranging papers analysing issues such as the risk of nuclear terrorism[1] and others that were specifically concerned with the response of the United States of America to the 9/11 attacks.[2]

The immediate response of the USA was centred on the termination of the Taliban regime in Afghanistan, seen as sponsors and supporters of the al-Qaeda movement that was charged with organising the attacks. The Taliban regime was terminated within three months of 9/11 and this was seen as a major achievement in countering and controlling al-Qaeda, although fighting in Afghanistan persisted into 2002, with particularly intensive interactions in the early months of that year at Tora Bora.

Even so, the rapid destruction of the regime was initially seen as representing major progress in achieving greater security for the USA, and a forceful US military posture was developed that encompassed two largely new elements. The first, enunciated in President George W. Bush's State of the Union address in January 2002, was the identification of an 'axis of evil' of rogue states that were distinguished by their support for international terrorism and their pursuit of weapons of mass destruction. The primary candidates for this status were Iraq, Iran and North Korea, with Syria, Libya and Cuba identified as lesser threats.

The second element was developed in President Bush's West Point speech three months later, when he emphasised the right of the USA to pre-empt future threats, by military action where necessary. While pre-emption forms a part of military strategy in many circumstances and by different countries, the forceful development of such a policy by the USA was clearly in the context of the war on terror and the linking of rogue states to support for terrorism and the development of weapons of mass destruction.

Within a year of the attacks, in the latter part of 2002, there was mounting evidence that the USA was preparing for military action against one member of the axis of evil, the regime of Saddam Hussein in Iraq. While this was apparently concerned with eliminating Iraq's presumed programmes to develop and deploy weapons of mass destruction, it seemed likely that the intended military action would go far beyond this to encompass regime termination. Such action was therefore likely to involve a substantial military campaign involving large-scale use of air power coupled with a ground invasion of the country by US forces working together with forces from other countries, most notably the United Kingdom.

Consequences of a War

There was concern among analysts working with the Oxford Research Group that such a military action could have grave consequences, and a briefing paper was therefore produced outlining such concern. *Iraq: Consequences of a War*, was published in October 2002, five months before the start of the war, and concluded that there were three major concerns that made it dangerous to terminate the regime by the use of force.[3]

The first was the risk of high civilian casualties. There were indications that the relatively short war in Afghanistan a year earlier had cost several thousand civilian lives, and the report also pointed to one US assessment that, in the event of a war with Iraq, there could be around 10,000 deaths among the Iraqi military and a further 10,000 civilian deaths.[4]

The second concern related to the numerous reports made available in Washington and London that the Iraqis had active programmes for the development and deployment of chemical and biological weapons (CBW). If these had even some degree of accuracy, then there was a risk that a regime threatened with termination might use such weapons systems as a last resort. The report argued that such a circumstance carried major dangers, including the possible escalation to the use of nuclear weapons by coalition military forces in response to Iraqi use of CBW in the context of attempted regime termination.

Given the nature of statements made by some US and UK officials in the run-up to the war, this appeared to be a reasonable assumption. At the same time, the report did not argue that Iraq was a major regional threat through its possible possession of chemical and biological weapons, but that regime termination in such circumstances had particular dangers that meant that using military force might therefore be singularly inappropriate.

The third issue that was raised in the report concerned the aftermath of a war. At the time of writing, there appeared to be a presumption in senior political circles in the USA and the UK that regime termination would be massively popular across Iraq, that the immediate post-war period would involve a high level of stability, the welcoming of foreign troops as liberators and the rapid establishment of a government friendly to the intervening powers. The report questioned this and pointed to two major dangers – the possible regional impact of a US occupation of Iraq across the Middle East and South West Asia, and the risk of an internal Iraqi insurgency.

On the first aspect, the report concluded that:

> The United States has sufficient forces to ensure regime destruction but the regime's replacement by occupying forces or by a client regime, even if the war is not greatly destructive, should be expected to increase regional opposition to the US presence. It is likely, in particular, to increase support for organisations such as al-Qaida and to prove counter-productive to peace and security in the region.

In relation to the risk of an internal Iraqi insurgency, the report said that:

> It is also possible that a paramilitary movement could develop from within Iraq. While there is abundant evidence of the unpopularity of the Saddam Hussein regime, it is certainly possible that internal opposition to

US occupation and the subsequent installing of a client regime would result in an evolving insurgency. Internal opposition to the current regime does not equate with the future acceptance of foreign occupation.

The overall conclusion of the report was:

Given these major consequences of war – high civilian casualties, risk of the use of weapons of mass destruction and post-war regional instability – alternatives to war should be sought as a matter of urgency.

Prior to the start of the war, there were other analysts with broadly similar concerns and there was also a substantial mobilisation of public opinion across the world, including a series of demonstrations on 15 February 2003 that involved many millions of people in numerous countries. Nevertheless, the war went ahead and the initial results seemed to suggest that those people who had attempted a critical analysis of the dangers of war had been proved wrong. Most notably, President Bush made a speech on 1 May 2003, on the flight deck of the aircraft carrier USS *Abraham Lincoln*, declaring major military operations over. Under a 'Mission Accomplished' banner, he looked forward to the establishment of a new government in Baghdad with, at most, minor problems of insecurity still to be dealt with.

Major combat operations have ended. In the battle for Iraq, the United States and our allies have prevailed. And now the coalition is engaged in securing and reconstructing the country.

In this battle, we have fought for the cause of liberty, and for the peace of the world. Our nation and our coalition are proud of this accomplishment – yet it is you, the members of the United States military, who achieved it. Your courage, your willingness to face danger for your country and for each other, made this day possible. Because of you, our nation is more secure. Because of you, the tyrant has fallen, and Iraq is free.

Although the mood in Washington and London was therefore positive, there were already clear indications that the situation in Iraq was beginning to deteriorate. In the weeks immediately after the termination of Saddam Hussein's regime, there was widespread lawlessness and looting, especially in Baghdad and Basra. Furthermore, there were early indications of the development of a guerrilla campaign directed against the occupying/ liberating forces. Moreover, there had actually been relatively few occasions, outside of the Kurdish areas of northeast Iraq, where there had been much rejoicing or welcoming of the foreign troops. Even the iconic destruction of a statue of Saddam Hussein in a Baghdad square involved no more than a few hundred people, with the statue itself actually being pulled down by US military personnel.

The Oxford Research Group Briefings

In these circumstances, and as one of its contributions to the analysis of global security trends, the Oxford Research Group therefore started a series of monthly briefings on international security with the main emphasis being on US security policy, primarily as it was being applied in Iraq but also in the context of the wider war on terror. The assessments started in May 2003 and were written and published on the ORG website within a five-to-seven-day period at the end of each month.[5] Over the first year, the ORG built up a body of analysis that gave a series of specific real-time perspectives on key trends. At the end of the year, the first twelve assessments were published, together with an overview analysis.[6] The present volume comprises the second year of these reports combined with a supporting discussion.

As with the first volume in this series, the monthly analyses are reproduced here as published – subject only to grammatical corrections and minor editorial changes to minimise repetition – and therefore give a series of specific real-time perspectives on key trends. As such they differ from the analysis of past events in that they attempt to give an indication of the main parameters in evidence at the time of writing. Such an approach has both disadvantages and advantages. Of the former, such immediate analysis may fail to identify significant long-term trends, or else these may only emerge with time. Also, it does not have the benefit of documentation and other forms of information relating to particular events or trends that might only emerge much later.

At the same time, by concentrating on immediate analysis, the monthly reports highlight particular aspects that may be lost from a later perspective. In particular, they are able to demonstrate what were thought to be key features of a chain of events at the particular time, features that may be neglected in subsequent studies yet help to explain the driving forces involved in the conflict.

This book therefore attempts to combine two forms of analysis, the monthly assessments and a more general review. In doing so, the emphasis is on the developing war in Iraq, but this is placed in a more general context of the conduct of the war on terror, not least in Afghanistan, as well as developments in the Israeli-Palestinian confrontation.

Chapter 1

Regime Termination and the Evolving War

T he first volume in this series charted the development of the war from the beginning of May 2003 to the end of April 2004, one year after President Bush's speech on the *USS Abraham Lincoln*.[1] In doing so, it sought to throw light on the reasons for the failure of regime termination to bring about the desired stability in Iraq, and to draw attention to features of the first three weeks of the conflict that were not clear at the time. Four aspects are now seen to be particularly relevant to the later development of the Iraq war, now in its third year.

The first concerns the role of elite Iraqi forces and their substantive absence from the main areas of fighting. The ordinary Iraqi Army played little role in the war. It largely comprised poorly equipped conscript troops that had little motivation for combat, and many of them were in under-strength and disorganised units that melted away in the face of the coalition attack. A more effective force was made up of several tens of thousands of the Republican Guard. In spite of some years of sanctions, these troops had some potential for resistance to occupation and some Republican Guard divisions were engaged by US forces south of Baghdad.

The divisions formed what amounted to an outer perimeter for the city of Baghdad, but were deployed at a distance from the urban areas and were subject to the full use of US firepower, including the substantial use of area-impact munitions such as cluster bombs and multiple rocket launchers. The Republican Guard units deployed in these circumstances suffered severe casualties and largely lost their coherence within days of engaging with US forces.

In the 1991 war, the eight divisions of the Republican Guard had formed the elite forces dedicated to regime survival, and most of this force was not actually engaged in the conflict in and around Kuwait, probably being held back to protect the regime in its heartland should the international coalition extend its operations towards Baghdad. By 2003, though, the Republican Guard was no longer the elite regime-protection force it had previously been, partly due to issues of reliability and loyalty that had arisen during the mid-1990s. Instead, a more restricted force, the Special Republican Guard, had been formed, and a number of Iraq's security and intelligence organisations, of which the regime had at least five, also had their own special forces. In addition, there were commando and *fedayeen* units that were considered to be loyal to the regime. All of these military formations together made up a considerable force – well over 20,000 in number.

There is little evidence that the Special Republican Guard units took any serious part in the conflict with coalition troops.

In particular, they appear to have dispersed by the time of the US occupation of Baghdad, with very little city-centre fighting following more violent action near the city's international airport during the third week of the war. It remains unclear whether there was a deliberate policy of withdrawal in preparation for a guerrilla phase of the campaign, or whether the withdrawal was disorganised and even partly due to elements of the Special Republican Guard leadership being bribed to order their troops to withdraw. It is possible that a combination of factors was at work, but the net effect was that a substantial force of elite troops took little part in the fighting and was therefore available for action at a later stage, following the occupation of the country by the USA and its coalition partners.

The second aspect of the war that is now seen to be more indicative of subsequent events was the development of violent responses by largely irregular forces during the first three weeks of the war. US forces and their coalition allies had little difficulty in moving their units across open country, meeting very little opposition in the process. They also had overwhelming firepower for defeating conventional Iraqi Army units, especially the Republican Guard, when these were deployed outside of urban areas.

What proved more difficult to counter were the numerous occasions when small paramilitary and military units engaged coalition forces in urban areas, or else undertook attacks on lightly guarded convoys on the open road. Although that part of the war leading to regime termination lasted only three weeks, the problem of 'irregular' opposition was, at times, serious, with many of the US casualties arising from such incidents. With the benefit of hindsight, it now seems clear that these incidents were 'markers' for the future. Even with the rapid movement of

US forces towards Baghdad, it was possible for Iraqi groups to mount irregular yet costly attacks on US and other forces, and to do so without immediately encountering opposition from an indigenous population that had been expected to welcome the occupying forces as liberators.

That there was not a widespread welcoming of liberation is the third notable characteristic of the early weeks of the war. Given the support that the Saddam Hussein regime had in the largely Sunni areas of central Iraq, there was little expectation that regime termination would be welcomed there. In other respects it was also confidently expected that the Kurdish region of north-east Iraq certainly would welcome regime termination, and this indeed proved to be the case.

What was surprising, and indeed discouraging to coalition forces, was the lack of welcome in those substantial parts of central Iraq and almost the whole of the south-east of the country that were populated primarily by Shi'a communities. Explanations were sought and three were offered. One was that the failure to detain Saddam Hussein and most of his leadership, including his sons Uday and Qusay, meant that there was a possibility that the regime could return, with the consequent fear that such a risk involved. This is reasonable in the context of the violent suppression of the Shi'a revolts after the 1991 war, and the lack of international support for the rebels at that time, but does not explain the lack of enthusiasm for 'liberation' in the months that were to follow.

The second was that elements of the regime were surviving in most of the towns and cities of southern Iraq, and that these elements were sufficiently strong to intimidate local populations, ensuring that they did not provide any support for coalition forces. Again, there may be an element of truth in this but, if so, it demonstrates a resilience among supporters of the former regime that should have been recognised as indicating the potential for a longer-term resistance to foreign occupation.

Finally, the immediate aftermath of regime termination included widespread and large-scale looting and criminal disorder, especially in Baghdad and Basra. Coalition forces were quite unable to maintain public order, and the Iraqi police forces largely withdrew from the major centres of population. The immediate chaos did much to blunt the impact of regime termination on public opinion across much of Iraq, suggesting that the US forces and their allies were far less in control than might have been expected.

The fourth aspect of the war that was largely missed during the early weeks was the extraordinarily wide distribution of supplies of arms and munitions across Iraq prior to the outbreak of the war. It became evident within weeks of the termination of the regime that there had been substantial military stockpiles, in scores if not hundreds of locations, established over a considerable period of time. In the immediate aftermath of the fall of Saddam Hussein's regime, there was no possibility of the relatively limited numbers of coalition troops securing these military supplies and this, combined with the melting away of many of the old regime's elite forces, meant that there could be further rapid dispersal.

It may seem surprising that this aspect of the old regime's behaviour had been missed, but it was, in all probability, an example of a misguided military mindset. During the course of the 1990s, there had been substantial periods of instability for the Saddam Hussein regime, with reports of regular purges of suspect officers and officials, even extending to the formation of an inner elite force, the Special Republican Guard, as mentioned earlier. In such circumstances there was an external assumption that the regime would maintain a relatively small number of large arms depots that could be closely guarded by reliable forces. A more widespread dispersal would make it more possible for dissident elements to gain access and possibly threaten the regime.

That the regime felt able to maintain a much more dispersed system of military logistical support suggests that it was actually rather more secure than had been anticipated. It also suggests that there was a resilience in support for the regime that might well survive an occupation by foreign forces. Whatever the accuracy of such an assessment, it was certainly the case that the sheer size of the dispersed arsenals was of great advantage to the forces opposing occupation as the insurgency began to develop within a few weeks of regime termination.

The Iraq War – Year 1

The implication of George W. Bush's 1 May speech on the *USS Abraham Lincoln* was that there would be relatively little insecurity in Iraq in the following months. US casualties in March and April 2003 had been relatively light, given that many thousands of Iraqi military and civilians were killed, with just sixty-five and seventy-four killed respectively, but, as the following figures show, the next twelve months were to be far more problematic than had been expected:

US Military Fatalities in Iraq[2]

May (2004)	37
June	30

July	48
August	35
September	31
October	44
November	82
December	40
January (2005)	47
February	20
March	52
April	135

Furthermore, the number of serious injuries suffered by US troops was very much higher in relation to the deaths than had been typical of past wars. In most twentieth-century conflicts, the ratio of those killed to those seriously injured was around 1:2 or 1:3, depending partly on the nature of the conflict but also on the extent of medical and evacuation services. The better such services were, the fewer soldiers would die relative to those surviving with serious injuries. In the Iraq conflict, US troops have had unusually high levels of combat medical support coupled with the use of armoured vehicles and, in particular, body armour.

As a result of these factors, survival rates have been much higher than in previous combats, but with many more soldiers suffering serious injuries, especially head, throat and groin injuries as well as wounds requiring the amputation of limbs. From the information that has been available, the ratio of deaths to serious injuries has been around 1:7, meaning that many thousands of US troops have suffered injuries likely to have a life-long effect. With troops in the field well aware of this somewhat hidden cost of the war, it should not be surprising that, when engaging in urban combat with irregular forces, US troops should use heavy firepower with consequent collateral civilian casualties.

During the course of the first year of the war there were several occasions when events suggested that the developing insurgency might wither away. Three of these stand out. The first was the killing of Uday and Qusay Hussein in Mosul in July 2003, but this had virtually no impact on the insurgency. Then, in November 2003, US military sources reported with some confidence that the insurgency was essentially being controlled by a handful of extended family networks operating in what was termed the Sunni heartland, and that these were capable of being brought under control. The following month, Saddam Hussein was detained and there was real confidence that the insurgency would die away. Neither of these developments had any substantive effect, and the insurgency gathered pace.

The extent of the insurgency contrasted markedly with US military expectations and with the political and economic planning being developed by the Coalition Provisional Authority (CPA) under the leadership of Paul Bremer. Until June 2004, the CPA was the effective government and administration of the country, and it was marked by a number of features. One was the determination to privatise much of the previously regime-controlled economy, with this allied to the introduction of a flat-rate income tax. A second feature was the process of 'de-Ba'athification' – the removal of those in public service who had been associated with the Ba'ath Party of the Saddam Hussein era. Parallel with this was the disbanding of the old army, a process the effectively put several hundred thousand young men into unemployment.

One of the issues with de-Ba'athification was that most senior and experienced civil servants had essentially been required to be members of the Ba'ath Party, whatever their personal political views, in order to retain their posts. By dismissing them, the CPA was removing much of a cohort of experienced public servants who had the capability to maintain a wide range of educational, health and other public services. Their removal onto the economic margins was deeply resented, as was the disbanding of the army.

Three of the more military aspects of the immediate post-war situation were also relevant to the longer-term development of the conflict. One of these was the work of the Iraq Survey Group which was set up in 2003 to survey and report on the old regime's presumed programme for the development and deployment of weapons of mass destruction (WMD). Although the Group carried on working for well over a year, it was clear within months of the termination of the old regime that nothing of substance was being found. In spite of extensive investigations involving hundreds of personnel, there was no substantive evidence of any WMD programme.

This did not have much bearing on the deteriorating situation in Iraq, but it did have a political impact in some of those countries that had supported the USA in taking military action to terminate the Saddam Hussein regime. This was most marked in the United Kingdom, where Tony Blair had argued forcefully that it was the WMD aspect of the regime's behaviour that was the security threat that justified the war.

A second military aspect was the confident expectation in Washington that substantial troop withdrawals would be possible within months of the occupation of the country. Figures suggested in the early months of 2003 had been of the order of a halving of troop deployments to around 70,000 by September 2003. At the same time, there were other indications that there would be a substantial long-term presence of US troops through the establishment of a number of permanent bases.[3] What seems likely is that the intention was to have perhaps four large bases in key parts of Iraq, with one near the capital city of Baghdad, one close to the major oil reserves in the south-east of the country and another along the Kirkuk-Mosul axis in the north, in Iraq's other major oil-bearing region. The fourth and final base would be in western Iraq, close to the Syrian border but also in the region where, it was suspected, the largest new oil reserves were likely to be found.

The combination of these developments – a free-market economy, a long-term military presence and internal security maintained without the need for occupying forces, would ensure that Iraq functioned as an exceptionally close ally of the USA over a timescale measured in decades rather than years. Given that Iraq has around four times the oil reserves of the entire USA, including Alaska, this would mean that US influence in the region could be stabilised, even in the face of political and social uncertainties in Saudi Arabia, and a regime in Iran that had very poor relations with the USA.

'Bring 'em On'

By the middle of 2003, it was already apparent that many aspects of the US plan for Iraq were deeply flawed. De-Ba'athification was seriously damaging reconstruction efforts, the dismantling of the army was providing a source of support for the oppositional elements, weapons of mass destruction were nowhere to be found, and an insurgency was developing that was proving difficult to counter. An added problem was that Islamic paramilitaries from other countries in the region, especially Saudi Arabia, were moving into Iraq to join with indigenous insurgents.

At one level, this was useful for the Bush administration in that it was possible to argue that the insurgency was, to a substantial extent, a phenomenon not rooted in Iraq but imported from elsewhere. It could further be argued that Iraq was therefore part of the wider global war on terror. There was a certain irony in this argument, since elements within the Bush administration had long argued that a subsidiary but significant argument for regime termination was the linkage between the Saddam Hussein regime and the al-Qaeda movement. Others had disputed this, not least because the regime was primarily secular in outlook for most of its period in office and had been criticised for this by Osama bin Laden, and the weight of evidence prior to the start of the war was that linkages between the regime and al-Qaeda were minimal at most.

It was only after the regime had been terminated and Iraq occupied by western forces that the country really did link in to the wider war on terror, as it became a focus of attention for Islamic radicals. From the perspective of supporters of movements such as al-Qaeda, Iraq was a major Arab country that was now occupied by neo-Christian forces that were closely allied to Zionist Israel. Moreover, the main long-term aim of the al-Qaeda movement was to establish an Islamic governance in the region that bore some similarities to the historic caliphates of past eras; the fact that Baghdad, the seat of the most notable caliphate, the Abbasids, was now occupied by foreign forces, gave an additional motive for aiding opposition.

Although the presence of foreign Islamic paramilitary forces in Iraq was not substantial during the first year of the war, there was a marked tendency in Washington to over-emphasise their presence, even to the extent of saying that Iraq now represented the core geographical region for the conduct of the war on terror. In the words of George W. Bush, the aim was to 'bring 'em on', in the sense that they would congregate in Iraq and there be eliminated. A central part of the war on terror would therefore be fought 6,000 miles away from the USA.

To put it in a crude manner, this outlook was known as the 'flypaper' theory of counter-terrorism, with Iraq being the flypaper, the incoming al-Qaeda affiliates being the flies and the US military capabilities being the insecticide. By the end of the first year of the war, the roles were, to an extent, being reversed. Moreover, al-Qaeda and its affiliates were maintaining a high level of activity in many parts of the world, including Indonesia, Turkey, Morocco, Saudi Arabia and Spain.[4]

In summary, a year after the termination of the Saddam Hussein regime, the transition to a stable client state with a permanent US military presence was proving very difficult and an insurgency was still evolving in spite of the presence of around 170,000 US and coalition troops in Iraq. Even so, the USA persisted with plans to appoint a provisional Iraqi administration from June 2004, with elections for an interim administration to be held during the winter months of 2004–2005, and there was some confidence that the insurgency could be controlled and that Iraqi security forces could be recruited and trained to take over most of the functions being undertaken by the USA and its coalition partners.

If such a process could be maintained, then it was presumed that the war would come to an end and the major elements of the original US policy towards Iraq could be implemented. Given that the period 2004–2005 also coincided with a US presidential election, this would be perhaps the key year in determining the long-term prospects for US policy towards Iraq and the wider region. In the chapters that follow, a contemporary analysis of the main features of the twelve months from May 2004 to April 2005 is presented, followed by a wider thematic discussion of the major developments of that period and their long-term implications.

Chapter 2
Problems on Two Fronts
May 2004

The difficulties faced by US forces in Iraq have yet to have a major impact on domestic politics in the USA, not least because Senator Kerry's campaign team is cautious about excessive criticism of George W. Bush for fear of appearing unpatriotic. One effect of this is to give Mr Bush a certain breathing space, and the apparent handover to an Iraqi administration may also help by giving the impression of the creation of an independent Iraq.[1]

In practice, it becomes increasingly apparent that a tightly controlled client regime in Baghdad is now being developed, led by Prime Minister Iyad Alawi with his previous links with western intelligence agencies. There will theoretically be a handover from the Coalition Provisional Authority under Paul Bremer, but the new US Embassy will be the world's largest, US personnel will dominate the country's development, and security will remain under the control of the US military.

To an extent, though, the impression can be given of a handover to a civil power, perhaps even with a short-term assumption that there will be a decline in the violence. The supporting evidence for this, though, is minimal. During the course of May, US forces only ended the violence in Fallujah by consolidating a truce that effectively made the city a 'no-go' area for coalition troops, leaving the city under the control of local militia.

Najaf, too, was not occupied, although one US military action there is likely to have long-term implications. This was the protracted and damaging exchange of fire in and around the vast cemetery close to the main mosque. There appears to have been no understanding on the part of the US military commanders that engaging in combat and using substantial firepower in such a sacred area would have a profound long-term effect on Shi'ite opinion.[2]

US commanders would say that they had no alternative, given the probable location of paramilitaries in the cemetery, but this is not the point. Such members of militias may well use cemeteries and mosques for shelter, but that in no way diminishes the impact of occupying forces fighting their way through these areas. To be colloquial, US forces may object to fighting with one hand tied behind their back, but that is exactly the nature of the predicament they now face in Iraq.

In the Sadr City district of Baghdad, unrest and conflict continued throughout May, and it is probable that the death toll among the Shi'ite communities during the month was close to a thousand. Coalition troops, especially Americans, took heavy casualties as well,[3] as did Iraqi police and civil defence units, but additional concerns were being raised in two quite different ways by the end of the month.

Economic Targeting

The first concern relates to the potential for insurgents to have a much greater impact on Iraqi reconstruction.[4] Over the past few months it has become clear that the insurgents may well be divided into a number of groups, yet they have a capacity for action that is much greater than had been realised. Many are drawn from Shi'ite militants, others may have links with the old Ba'ath party, some stem from small radical Islamic groups that were already operating in Iraq, some represent a new type of Iraqi nationalism, and there are also some foreign paramilitaries now operating in the country.

The extent to which different groups may cooperate is far from clear, but their levels of organisation are considerable and they could yet coalesce into a broadly based uprising. The various groups still have access to large quantities of munitions, many of them secreted away in the past year from the arsenals held by the old regime. While some of the Shi'ite militia may not have had much in the way of military training, many others, especially from the Sunni communities, were involved in the Special Republican Guard and brigades attached to the old security agencies, and those paramilitaries entering Iraq from elsewhere will almost certainly have appropriate training. Meanwhile, the new Iraqi army is not proving reliable in its support for US forces, and the police force continues to be subject to repeated attacks.

Behind all this lies a real fear within the Coalition Provisional Authority that some of the insurgents are biding their time and have the capacity to cause much greater economic destruction than they have so far tried to do. In particular, there is a suspicion that insurgents have actually been holding back from attacking electricity supplies, and their targeting of oil facilities has been far below their capabilities.

It follows that there may be a more substantive strategy at work – the withholding of some insurgent actions until closer to the date of the theoretical handover of power. If this is the case, then the key period is going to be the three months from June to August. This will be at the height of the summer heat, when a new government is taking control, and when Iraq most needs its oil revenues. Recent insecurity has already had a massive effect on reconstruction, with many projects on hold. A further upsurge in attacks could destabilise any new government, forcing the US military planners to take on a more high-profile security role and therefore demonstrating to people in Iraq and beyond that a client regime is in place in Baghdad and that it is the USA that is really calling the shots.[5]

Saudi Arabia

Such potential instability links in with the second issue – what is already happening in Saudi Arabia. Here, the past two months has seen an upsurge in attacks from paramilitary groups at least loosely related to al-Qaeda, including an attack on an oil industry company in Yanbu and the killing of a German expatriate in Riyadh. Most significant of all was the attack on a series of offices in Khobar, at the heart of the Saudi oil industry, followed by hostage taking in a well-protected residential compound.[6]

Given the dispersal of the Saudi oil industry, none of this means an immediate disruption of exports, but the longer-term significance is very much in the direction of uncertainty in the international oil markets. Perhaps the key issue is whether the events in Iraq and Saudi Arabia are connected. This could be in the form of a degree of planning and coordination by strategists within al-Qaeda, or else it could be more a matter of common cause, with no one person or group at the centre.

On balance, it is more likely to be the latter, and this has considerable implications for the USA and its coalition partners. If there is a degree of central organisation behind current developments in Iraq and Saudi Arabia, then it may be possible to pre-empt some actions or at least acquire intelligence on the strategy. If it is more amorphous and is arising more or less spontaneously from current circumstances, as seems to be the case, then responding in the conventional forms of counter-terrorism actions will be a further case of treating the symptoms while failing to address the causes. It is an approach that will remain as counter-productive as it has for almost the whole of the three years since 9/11.

Chapter 3
Transfer of Power or Client Regime?
June 2004

Towards the end of May, there was some respite in Iraq from the intense conflicts of the previous month, not least with a substantial decrease in the activities of most of the militias associated with Moqtada al-Sadr. There was also a temporary halt to the violence in the largely Sunni city of Fallujah, although the developments that took place there may have a longer-term significance for the future of the insurgency.[1]

Essentially, US marines refrained from the use of their overwhelming firepower against paramilitaries in the city, not least because the several hundred casualties and physical destruction of the previous month had been widely reported across the region and had also failed to bring about the defeat of the insurgents.

The situation was eased, at least for the time being, by a decision by US military commanders to allow an Iraqi military force drawn largely from the former Iraqi Army to take control of the city. This was, in a sense, an admission that the costs of US control of the city would be unacceptable, but the problem for the US military was that it quickly became apparent that the 'official' Iraqi units were working in close collaboration with the paramilitaries. During the course of June, Iraqi journalists were able to report that paramilitaries were running roadblocks, working with the Iraqi units and even seeking to impose religious laws on parts of the city. Fallujah was therefore effectively under the partial control of the insurgents and this was a situation that the USA was not in a position to counter.[2]

The Political Transition in Iraq

In Iraq as a whole, preparations for a handover to an appointed interim government were accelerated, and it became clear that this handover would have four significant elements. The first was that the pace of training of Iraqi police, civil defence and para-military forces would be increased, in the hope that they would take over many of the public-order and anti-insurgency functions previously in the hands of the coalition military forces.

The second element, following on directly from this, was that US military forces would seek to scale down the intensity of their own patrol activities, thereby reducing their exposure to attacks by insurgents. This could be a particularly important development for the Bush administration, given the domestic political significance of further casualties in an election year. The third element, though, was that there remained a determination to use considerable force whenever this was thought necessary, including substantial bombing attacks by strike aircraft against potential insurgent targets. Presumed insurgent locations in

Fallujah, for example, were subject to repeated attacks towards the end of June, often resulting in civilian casualties.

Finally, towards the end of the month, the nature of the interim government – the new regime of Prime Minister Alawi – was beginning to become clear, and it appeared to have many of the components of a client regime. In one of his final acts before departing, for example, the US head of the old Coalition Provisional Authority, Paul Bremer, ensured that inspectors-general were appointed to oversight roles in numerous Iraqi ministries. He also ensured that newly appointed heads of key security and intelligence offices would have five-year terms, thereby remaining in power whatever government might eventually be elected.[3]

Mr Bremer's effective successor is Ambassador John Negroponte, a highly experienced diplomat who, previously in his career, has overseen US operations in support of strongly pro-American governments in countries in Central America. In Iraq, Ambassador Negroponte will head the largest embassy of any country anywhere in the world. Furthermore, this will be an embassy with 200 staff allocated to Iraqi ministries and will also have four major regional centres and five sub-centres stretching across the country. It will, in other words, ensure a significant US presence throughout the Iraqi instruments of governance.

Coupled with an aid programme that is close to bankrolling many of the country's economic activities, it becomes apparent that a fully fledged client regime is being established. Moreover, early moves by the new regime have included the establishment of a range of emergency powers including provisions for martial law, and suggestions that the security situation may require a delay in the elections provisionally planned for early in 2005.

In effect, what has emerged is an Iraqi regime that maintains a remarkably close relationship with the USA, and seems set to do so for a prolonged period. Moreover, there are no indications of any withdrawal of US troops from Iraq, and there are reports that current troop levels of around 140,000 could actually be maintained for several years.[4] Coupled with continuing commitments in Afghanistan, this does much to explain the problems of overstretch facing the US military, problems that are requiring redeployment of US troops away from South Korea and preparations to call up several thousand more reservists.[5]

The NATO Summit

At the end of June, the introduction of the Alawi regime was brought forward two days, partly for security reasons but also because it then coincided with the NATO Heads of State meeting in Istanbul. While it was possible to represent the changes in Iraq as a move towards a possible democratic rule, the outcome of the NATO summit itself was less easy to present in a positive light.

The Bush administration had initially hoped for a clear commitment to increased numbers of troops for Iraq from NATO member states, not least to relieve pressure on its own forces. This commitment was not forthcoming and, more significantly in the circumstances, it was not even possible to persuade alliance members to allow NATO to take over the leadership of the multilateral coalition division operating in southern Iraq, a move which, from Washington's perspective, would at least have involved NATO formally in Iraq.

There is separate pressure on NATO, not least from President Hamid Karzai in Afghanistan, to increase its commitment to the International Security Assistance Force (ISAF), so that its remit can spread out beyond Kabul to other cities and also to main transport routes. In the event, nothing more than a very modest increase in commitments was forthcoming.

At one level, it is obvious that most Western European states are thoroughly anxious to avoid any increased commitments in Iraq, not least because of the uncertainty surrounding the intensity of the insurgency. While this may well be understandable, it is possible to level much more substantial criticism at European responses to the predicament in Afghanistan.

UN diplomats, Afghan government officials, NGO specialists and independent analysts are virtually unanimous in the view that Afghanistan is simply not getting the security and development assistance it urgently needs. Much of the country remains under the control of warlords, opium production has increased massively and parts of south-east and eastern Afghanistan remain subject to a persistent Taliban insurgency.[6]

The USA and some coalition partners are maintaining at least 15,000 troops in those latter parts of the country fighting a counter-insurgency war, but this has been made more difficult because the Pakistani Army, across the border, has had little success in curbing insurgent activity in its border regions.

The danger for the Karzai administration is that the continuing problems of instability, warlordism and chronic underdevelopment in the rest of Afghanistan will ensure that the power of the warlords remains and a democratic transition will therefore prove extremely difficult. It may even make it possible for a more general Taliban resurgence to develop. For these reasons alone, the failure of western states to offer greatly increased assistance appears remarkably short-sighted. In one small but significant move, though, there are some indications that the UK government might actually increase its commitment to ISAF rather than increase the troop numbers in Iraq. This appears, though, an exception to the rule within NATO.

Al-Qaeda in Saudi Arabia

During the course of June, paramilitary actions continued in Saudi Arabia and there were indications of a strategy emerging that is rather different from the presumed strategy of the al-Qaeda consortium towards the Kingdom. In terms of its general aims, the al-Qaeda group has three short-term perspectives and one overall aim, the entire strategy being seen as evolving over several decades. In the short term, there is the requirement to force foreign troops out of the western Gulf states, to bring about the downfall of the Royal House of Saud as the unacceptable Keeper of the Two Holy Places and, a more peripheral aim, to aid the creation of a Palestinian state. The longer-term aim is the establishment of 'acceptable' Islamist governance, initially across the Middle East, perhaps in the manner of a renewed caliphate.

The assumption among many analysts has been that much of the concentration of al-Qaeda's activities would be on the aim of destroying the House of Saud, but a strategy may now be emerging that is much more geared to producing a sense of insecurity in the Kingdom to the extent that the House of Saud is unable to cope. At the same time, and especially if there is a progressive withdrawal of western expatriates from the Kingdom, people sympathetic to al-Qaeda's aims might acquire greater power and influence within the Kingdom.[7]

This would amount to change from within rather than an attempt to instigate the violent overthrow of the Kingdom. The belief behind such a strategy is that violent overthrow would be bound to bring in a strong US military reaction, given the extraordinary importance of the Saudi oil supplies. While such a US intervention might spark a radical response, the ensuing instability could set back the economic development of the Kingdom and surrounding states. As such, it might be better to effect internal political change that might still have the longer-term outcome of the decline and fall of the House of Saud.

Israel and Iraq

In Israel, violence has continued, with by far the greatest loss of life in the last two months being experienced by the Palestinians, especially in Gaza. The harsh counter-insurgency actions of the Israeli Defense Forces continue to be widely reported across the Middle East, as do the strong links between the Israeli and US military in matters such as training and equipment for urban counter-insurgency operations. This tends to reinforce the view in much of the Arab world that a joint Israeli-American operation is in progress in the region, and this view is being further reinforced by reports of Israeli involvement in Kurdish areas of Iraq.

With the implied consent of the US occupying forces in the region, it appears that Israeli Special Forces have been active in training Kurdish military units, with this enabling an Israeli involvement to develop within Iraq. Motives for such an involvement may include the ability to support Kurds in Syria against the Syrian government, connections between Iraqi and Iranian Kurds leading to improved intelligence about Iranian nuclear ambitions, and increased influence in Kurdish Iraq itself with its substantial oil reserves.

There may also be a view in Israel that the US predicament in Iraq is unsustainable and that chaotic conditions may develop that could cause a degree of regional instability. In such circumstances, Israeli influence in the one ethnic group that has the most highly organised military forces, the Iraqi Kurds, could be of value to Israel itself.

The impact of such an Israeli involvement could be considerable. It is likely to cause substantial concern in neighbouring Iran, perhaps enabling the more rigid theocratic elements to consolidate power. It is also likely to further reinforce the wider Arab perception of exceptionally close links between Israel and the USA.

Overview

In seeking to gain a general perspective on developments in the Middle East, three issues have emerged recently. One is confirmation that the USA is retaining effective control of security in Iraq and has political influence over the Alawi government in Baghdad to the extent that it is a client regime. The second is the probable emergence of an al-Qaeda strategy for Saudi Arabia that may seek to avoid the violent overthrow of the House of Saud while gaining influence on Saudi governance to effect an increasing degree of control from within.

Finally, a significant if little-noticed development has been the involvement of Israel in the Kurdish areas of Iraq. This latter development may turn out to be the most significant of all, suggesting that US neoconservative thinking on the need for the region to be reshaped by the USA working in conjunction with Israel is a project that is very much in progress. The reaction to such a development may be slow in coming, but it may ultimately ensure a violent response that could see the instability in Iraq extend to involve both Iran and Syria.

Chapter 4
Iran Comes into the Frame
July 2004

Iraq

The US policy towards Iraq that became apparent in the run-up to the establishment of the Alawi regime (see June briefing, Chapter 3) was consolidated during the course of July. The elements of the policy were relatively complex but had the aim of ensuring a degree of stability in the country while attempting to avoid large numbers of US casualties.

The Alawi regime was duly established at the end of June, supported by a substantial US embassy, which effectively replaced the Coalition Provisional Authority. With senior officials appointed to every government ministry and with a number of regional offices, the Embassy has the capacity to oversee the evolution of the Alawi regime and its maintenance as a client state supported by around 140,000 US troops and up to 30,000 coalition troops from other countries, principally the UK, Poland, Ukraine and Italy.

US troops, in particular, have sought to reduce their presence in the form of routine patrols, but are willing to use substantial firepower, particularly from helicopters and fixed-wing aircraft, when considered necessary.[1] At the same time, determined efforts have been made to accelerate the training of Iraqi police and security forces in order to decrease the Alawi regime's dependence on US forces.[2]

In the first month of the new regime, there have been substantial indications that the policy is flawed and may be unworkable. If so, this is likely to mean considerable violence and suffering within Iraq in addition to a significant impact on domestic politics in the USA. One early indicator, for example, was that fifty-four US troops were killed in July compared with forty-two in June, and there was also a substantial increase in the number of injuries, with over 650 troops injured during the month, nearly 300 of them sustaining serious injuries.[3]

For the Iraqi authorities, July also marked a continuing pattern of kidnappings, car bombs, mortar and rocket attacks and many other forms of violence. Many of the attacks were directed against the police and civil defence forces but the trend towards the assassination of politicians and senior civil servants also continued.[4]

For the Alawi regime, perhaps the most serious problem is that neither it nor the US forces have control over a number of towns and cities in much of central Iraq. Since the intense fighting in Fallujah in April, that city and the surrounding towns and villages have effectively been under the control of insurgents.[5] Among supporters of the insurgents, both in Iraq and beyond, Fallujah is being seen as a 'liberated city' and is assumed by them to be the first of many.

In practice, there are already examples of other towns and cities, such as Samarra, where governmental control is minimal. Such a situation also exists in some major Shi'a centres of population including the large Sadr City slum area of Baghdad and the religious centre of Najaf. Some analysts are arguing that the Alawi regime, in reality, only has control of Baghdad and some of the surrounding towns, together with partial control of Basra. This is probably an exaggeration, but it does appear to be the case that the first month of the regime saw an increase in the loss of central control in Iraq as a whole.

Within the USA, the impact of the continuing violence has been relatively low. This is primarily because the domestic media interest in Iraq has diminished with the departure of the head of the CPA, Paul Bremer, the relatively low profile of his effective successor, Ambassador John Negroponte, and the installation of the Alawi regime.

At a superficial level, therefore, it can be argued that Iraq is no longer under US control, one of the results being a degree of media disinterest. This is similar to the attitude to Afghanistan, where US interest in aiding the civil reconstruction of that country is minimal and the emphasis remains on counter-insurgency.

Afghanistan

In spite of the lack of concern about Afghanistan in the USA as a whole, the situation within the country itself remains deeply problematic.[6] Warlords are in control of much of the country, opium poppy growing has expanded hugely and the Afghan government has only limited influence beyond Kabul. The International Security Assistance Force (ISAF) has been quite effective in supporting local security and police forces in the capital, and some Provincial Reconstruction Teams in other towns and cities have also had a positive effect.

External peacekeeping assistance has, however, been far below that required – most independent analysts see the need for a force of up to 30,000 troops, but even the expansion of ISAF that followed the NATO summit in Istanbul at the end of June will not take it above 10,000. Afghanistan is also lacking the level of civil assistance required, even if some progress is being made in areas such as voter registration.

Meanwhile, there are indications that the USA has further increased its counter-insurgency operations in the east and south-east of the country, with as many as 20,000 combat troops now stationed in the country, the largest force to be deployed there so far. Over the past six months, US forces have sought to work with Pakistani Army units, with the latter operating in border areas such as South Waziristan. In a number of military operations undertaken since March, Pakistani forces have attempted to disrupt Taliban and other movements. There have been some deaths or detentions of significant militants, but the effects have been far less than had been hoped or expected.

Indeed, there have been indications during June and July that the Taliban and other militia have become much more adept at operating in circumstances in which US forces can rely on a wide range of satellite and aerial reconnaissance systems backed up by helicopters and fixed-wing aircraft for rapid attacks against identified targets. The insurgents have responded by operating in small groups and engaging in short-term military actions designed to let them melt away rapidly into local populations.

On the one hand this means that a wholesale Taliban revival is difficult to envisage but, against this, even the most sophisticated counter-insurgency systems available to the USA do not seem able to bring the Taliban insurgency under control, even with the recent substantial troop reinforcements. The end result is that the USA is likely to find itself committed to a long-term military involvement in Afghanistan at a time of increasing overstretch in its forces, especially the US Army, where the call-up of further groups of reserves is now anticipated.

Iran

The June briefing reported the involvement of Israeli Special Forces in training Kurdish military units in north-east Iraq, further supporting the view across much of the Arab world that the termination of the Saddam Hussein regime was, to an extent, a US/Israeli operation – part of a long-term strategy of securing control of Arab oil. Whatever the truth of such a perception, there was also the issue of the impact of such Israeli involvement on political developments in Iran.

In the past two months, there has been a marked increase in the anti-Iranian rhetoric of elements of the Bush administration, with insistence that the policy of states such as Britain, France and Germany – engagement rather than confrontation – is failing in the face of continued Iranian commitments to nuclear weapons developments. Iranian officials continue to insist that they only have a civil nuclear power programme. The view within the Bush administration, however, is that conservative theocrats are firmly and fully in control in Tehran and that a key part of their policy is to use civil nuclear developments as a front for the rapid acquisition of nuclear weapons.[7]

The view of Iran as a major danger in the region is deep-seated in Washington and stretches well beyond the immediate neoconservative lobby within the Bush administration. It goes right back to the fall of America's close ally, the Shah of Iran, at the end of the 1970s, the rise of theocratic governance and, in particular, the Tehran hostage crisis in 1980 when over fifty US diplomats were held for many months by the new revolutionary regime.

Opposition to the Tehran regime was a prime reason for US support for Saddam Hussein during the latter stages of the Iran-Iraq war in 1986–1988, and current opposition stems also from a deeply held Israeli belief that Iran is its greatest threat in the entire region. Whether or not Iran is planning to develop nuclear weapons, though, it is useful to sense the perspective on the current crisis as seen from the viewpoint of conservative theocratic elements in Tehran. Given that the relatively reformist government in Tehran has failed to deliver those reforms demanded by many young Iranians, it is certainly the case that theocratic elements have considerable power within the country, and this is unlikely to diminish in the short term.

Ever since the period of the Shah's rule, the USA has been seen by such elements as wanting to maintain influence, if not indirect rule, in Iran. This perception has, in Iranian conservative eyes, reached a new peak since the installation of the Bush presidency in 2001 and the subsequent declaration of Iran as one of three members of the 'axis of evil'. Since then, one of the other members, the Saddam Hussein regime in Iraq, has been terminated by forceful military action.

Iran now finds itself with about 140,000 US troops on its immediate western borders, with many tens of thousands more troops in Kuwait and other western gulf states. It sees the reconstituted US Fifth Fleet operating unhindered in the Persian Gulf and the Arabian Sea, as well as having Afghanistan, immediately to the east, in a state of disarray which includes a further 20,000 US troops fighting a counter-guerrilla war. This is also in addition to instability in the Caucasus, where there is ongoing competition for pipeline routes, not least as the USA, in Tehran's eyes, seeks to limit the involvement of Iran in the transport of oil resources from the region.

Although away from Iran's immediate vicinity, recent US involvement in Central Asian republics such as Uzbekistan is seen as further proof of Washington's desire to exert control across the wider region. The final factor is the recent Israeli involvement in Iraq, right on Iran's north-west border, with this involvement being impossible without the active agreement of the USA.

Taking all these factors together, it is possible to get some understanding of what could be a strong Iranian perception of substantial vulnerability to external interference, if not a threat to the regime itself. There may well be a degree of paranoia in all of this – after all, the USA is hugely preoccupied in very difficult military situations in both Iraq and Afghanistan, and surely does not have time to take on Iran as well. Against this, though, is the increasingly strident rhetoric coming out of Washington, the Israeli presence in neighbouring Iraq and the risk of a military attack on Iranian nuclear facilities, by either the USA or Israel.

There is one further factor that is likely to be affecting Iranian attitudes. The third 'member' of the axis is North Korea, and this, too, has been the subject of strong rhetoric from Washington. Here, though, there is some evidence to suggest that North Korea has succeeded in putting together a very primitive nuclear arsenal, perhaps a handful of devices, and also has very strong conventional forces close to heavily populated parts of South Korea. North Korea appears to have gone ahead and supplemented conventional strength with a crude nuclear deterrent, and this has resulted in diminished rhetoric from Washington and an apparent determination to avoid a crisis, even to the extent of engaging in a degree of negotiation, possibly in concert with China.

To put it crudely, the view from Tehran may well be that North Korea is under less 'threat' than it was three years ago, whereas the vulnerability of Iran has increased. From such a perception, three policies would be expected to arise. One would be the rapid development of a deterrent capability, however crude and limited in extent. The second would be an attempt to do this in a thoroughly decentralised manner, making military pre-emption by the USA or Israel more difficult. The third would be to provide more aid to insurgents in Iraq in order to further preoccupy US forces in that country.

The problem is that any such options, however necessary from Tehran's perception, are precisely those options that will make it more likely that US or Israeli pre-emptive military action will actually take place. This could even be in the immediate run-up to the US presidential election in November.

In such a context, the Western European approach of seeking engagement with Tehran may currently be viewed with deep suspicion in Washington, but seems more likely to avoid an immediate crisis. This does not mean that it provides a long-term solution to the vexed problem of US/Iranian relations – there is certainly going to be a great deal of new thinking necessary for that. The alternative, though, is of a further extension of President Bush's war on terror to a new zone of conflict with every risk of further instability and conflict in the Persian Gulf region.

Chapter 5
A Change of Direction?
August 2004

The international news media in August were dominated by three weeks of intense fighting in the Iraqi holy city of Najaf, but the conflict there formed just one part of a wider problem of insurgency in Iraq which, in turn, was paralleled by events in Israel, Afghanistan, Nepal and Russia.[1]

In Iraq itself, August was the second full month of the provisional Alawi government, with substantial US influence stretching throughout its ministries and through the regions (see Chapters 3 and 4). Around 140,000 US troops remain in Iraq, supported by over 20,000 troops from other countries, but their continuing presence is accompanied by intensive efforts to train a large new Iraqi police force, together with border guards, a civil defence force and a small regular army. In addition, there are reported to be many thousands of foreign private security personnel operating throughout the country.

Najaf

Although the siege and violence in Najaf was just one part of a wider problem of insurgency, its development and the manner of its ending have an enduring significance for the country for a number of reasons. One, undoubtedly, is the manner in which the peace agreement fronted by Grand Ayatollah Sistani has increased his own status and authority, but allied to this is the very extent of the insurgency. This was not restricted to Najaf but affected towns and cities across southern Iraq as well as the large Sadr City district of Baghdad.[2]

Moreover, the real significance of the fighting in Najaf, as with earlier Shi'ite actions there and in many other parts of Iraq earlier in the year, is the remarkable way in which many people within the Iraqi Shi'a majority have moved, over the past year, to fervent opposition to US occupation.[3]

The contrast between initial US expectations for post-war Iraq and the actual events is stark. Across much of central and northern Iraq, Sunni insurgents are maintaining a high level of activity against US troops and the Iraqi civil authorities. US forces have suffered close to 1,000 killed since the start of the war, with many thousands of injuries, 1,100 in August alone. Attacks on US forces during August were running at sixty per day, a one-fifth increase on the three months up to the end of June, and kidnappings of foreigners and attacks on the energy infrastructure show no signs of diminishing. A particular additional feature has been a series of attacks on senior Iraqi politicians, civil servants and academics, and persistent attacks on Iraqi police stations and police officers.

It is in addition to this, though, that the Shi'ite rebellions have been so significant, given that there was such confidence in Shi'a support for US forces. Four factors are relevant in analysing the development of this rebellion and its possible further implications. One is that it stems, in part, from the relative marginalisation of many Shi'a communities in major urban areas, a process made more extreme by the lack of employment opportunities and the very slow pace of reconstruction. This is made worse by the frequent use of migrant labour from South Asia, particularly for sensitive transport and construction projects.

A second factor has been the relative success of Shi'a militia in maintaining control of key parts of Najaf in the face of an assault from heavily armed and well-protected US troops.[4] It is true that the US forces were constrained initially from damaging the extensive Valley of Peace cemetery and later from attacking the main shrine, but later during the conflict they were prepared to use heavy ordnance in the cemetery and in the crowded city streets surrounding the shrine, utilising tanks, armoured fighting vehicles, AC-130 gunships, attack helicopters and strike aircraft to cause massive damage in both areas.

Even with these deployments, and with some 3,000 troops facing the much smaller Mehdi Army, a radical Shi'a militia, it proved very difficult for US forces to make much progress in their aim of defeating Moqtada al-Sadr's forces. Eventually, the US forces were ready and willing to accept the ceasefire facilitated by the return of Ayatollah Sistani from the UK, even though it meant their withdrawal from Najaf in circumstances that allowed many of the surviving militia to slip away, with weapons and munitions dispersed, as well as the survival of Moqtada al-Sadr himself.

What has to be recognised is that these militia were very largely untrained and thoroughly inexperienced in urban guerrilla warfare and were equipped primarily with light arms extending up to light mortars and rocket-propelled grenades. Even so, they were sufficiently determined to be able to sustain substantial casualties in the face of much more massive US firepower and to do so for three weeks.

The third factor is that during the conflict in Najaf, more details emerged of Sunni insurgents supporting the Shi'a militia, and of the willingness of experienced paramilitaries from Fallujah and elsewhere being prepared to travel to Najaf and Sadr City to train Shi'a insurgents in urban warfare.[5] Although there was a relative degree of peace by the end of August, for the more radical Shi'a militia the end result had been the acquiring of substantial experience in the methods of rebellion and the belief that a victory of sorts had been achieved, in that the overwhelming military power of the US forces had not enabled them to evict the militia. A subsidiary aspect of this was the perceived failure of the Alawi regime to negotiate a settlement at any stage in the conflict, a failure compounded by a degree of propaganda concerning the supposed progress of US and Iraqi forces that came close, at times, to being incredible.

The fourth and final factor is one that stems partly from the Najaf siege but also from the more general tactics used by US forces in Najaf and elsewhere in Iraq. A pattern has emerged in which US forces are located primarily in secure fortress-like centres and go on patrol in body armour, travelling in Bradley armoured vehicles, armoured Humvees and tanks. There is heavy and frequent use of ground-based firepower but this is now regularly accompanied by the use of attack helicopters, AC-130 gunships and strike aircraft.

The point here is that such use of firepower has become much more general, especially since the conflict at Fallujah in April. That city has since been subject to frequent air strikes, as have many other towns. Such actions are repeatedly said to be aimed at targets such as 'safe houses' that may be occupied by insurgents, but there is abundant evidence of frequent civilian casualties. US authorities regularly deny this, but the regional media such as the Al Jazeera and Al Arabiya satellite news channels provide ample coverage of this 'collateral damage'.

The US military command insists that it 'doesn't do body counts' of Iraqi insurgents and civilians, and it is therefore left to Iraqi sources and international non-governmental organisations to try and make reliable assessments. These, in turn, give the lie to the idea that Iraq has experienced a three-week war followed by an uneasy peace. One of the primary sources for civilian casualties, the Iraq Body Count Group (IBC), is now recording civilian deaths at over 12,000 since the war started, with casualty figures running at around 250 deaths per month, even in relatively 'quiet' months such as July.[6]

Asymmetric Warfare and the US Presidential Election

At the end of August, the Republican Party met in New York City to confirm George W. Bush as its candidate in the November presidential election. Over the past month or so, the Republican tactics have concentrated on damaging Senator Kerry's Vietnam War record and on promoting President Bush as the 'War President' in the face of a perceived and continuing threat from al-Qaeda and its affiliates.

This reached a peak in President Bush's acceptance speech and the current indications are that it is a workable strategy that is beginning to give him a lead in the election race, with the more vulnerable areas such as the economy and fiscal deficits being relegated to the sidelines if not ignored.

In parallel with the Convention, though, a series of incidents in Russia, Israel, Iraq and Afghanistan at the end of the month all served to cast doubt on the current approaches to the war on terror. The continued violence in Iraq may currently be having little domestic impact, and the bombings in Afghanistan scarcely get a mention in the mainstream US domestic media.

In Israel, too, the double bus bombing in Beersheba has been presented not as a reason to question the vigorous Israeli action against the Palestinian community but more as proof that even tougher action and the acceleration of the building of the wall along the boundary with the West Bank to deter suicide bombers are the appropriate responses.

In Russia, too, there remains a tendency to support President Putin in his anti-Chechen actions, even if they appear now to be creating a new generation of thoroughly radicalised Chechen rebels. A spate of violence over the past three months rose to a new peak at the end of August with the destruction of two airliners, a suicide bombing at a Moscow Metro station and the siege of a school at Beslan in North Ossetia, ending in chaotic scenes with the loss of well over 300 lives, many of them children, and injuries to many hundreds more. In all, Russia suffered close to 500 civilian deaths and far more injuries in a series of actions that, even in Russia, began to raise doubts about Mr Putin's policies.

Such doubts were more firmly expressed in Western Europe, to the anger of the Russian government, and were in contrast to Mr Putin's insistence that the Chechen rebels were linked to al-Qaeda and that his forceful actions in Chechnya were therefore a legitimate part of the international war on terror.

Within Republican circles in the USA, there is some hesitation in supporting Mr Putin too openly, partly because of a persistent suspicion of Russia that dates back to the cold war era. At the same time, the horror of the Beslan school siege is such that it serves as a powerful reminder of the threat of terrorism and therefore adds to a sense of threat that is believed to represent an asset to Mr Bush's re-election prospects.

Rebirth of the 'Present Danger'

Perhaps most indicative of neoconservative thinking in the USA is the reconstitution of the Committee on the Present Danger, the third time that its supporters have seen the need for such a movement.[7] The Committee was formed in the USA in the early 1950s and did much to convince Americans of the dangers of the Soviet threat. It receded into the background in the 1960s and early 1970s but was brought back to life in the last few years of the 1970s during the presidency of Jimmy Carter.

Along with groups such as High Frontier and the Heritage Foundation, the Committee on the Present Danger played a major role in elevating the Soviet threat to a key issue in the 1980 presidential election, aided by the Soviet intervention in Afghanistan and the Iranian revolution and hostage crisis. Ronald Reagan formed an administration in 1981 that involved many members of the Committee in security-related posts; there was a substantial increase in defence budgets and a more aggressive attitude to the Soviet Union. When the cold war finally ended, the Committee on the Present Danger once again receded into the shadows.

Now it has been reconstituted, involving a wide range of neoconservative and allied figures, many of them involved in the late 1970s incarnation. In its literature, the Committee has replaced the Soviet menace with an almost imperceptible change to the menace of Islamic fundamentalism, arguing that this is the greatest threat facing the USA and calling for greater defence spending and vigorous actions wherever required.

It is probable that the Committee has been reconstituted now in the light of a possible Kerry victory in the November election. Given the attitude of the Bush administration and its robust pursuit of al-Qaeda and the 'axis of evil', it is not easy to see the need for the Committee should President Bush be re-elected. A Kerry victory would be another matter, and there may well be a perceived need to have the necessary lobbying groups ready to ensure a thorough opposition to any liberalisation by a Kerry administration of the pursuit of rogue states and terrorists.

A Change of Direction?

The parallel problems in Najaf, and in Iraq more widely, in Afghanistan, in Israel and in Russia during August might be expected to call into question the overall policies currently being pursued by Israel, Russia and the USA. But there seems little sign of that, even if governmental and public opinion in Europe is far more circumspect.

With the USA being the lead actor in this war on terror, the signs of any change are minimal. A second term for President Bush might possibly involve some reconsideration but it seems unlikely, and the renewed Committee on the Present Danger, in concert with other policy groups, will argue forcefully against any change in policy by a Kerry administration. For now, the conclusion has to be that any rethinking of strategy and exploration of less militaristic approaches is unlikely, even given the difficulties experienced in August. Ultimately, new approaches may be forthcoming from Western Europe and elsewhere, but they are unlikely to make much headway for many months to come.

Chapter 6
Iraq and
a Wider War
September 2004

Much of the media emphasis on Iraq during August was concerned with the intense fighting in Najaf that was finally ended by the ceasefire agreement aided by Grand Ayatollah Sistani. It involved the withdrawal of Moqtada al-Sadr's militia but also of US military forces. Security was turned over to Iraqi police and paramilitary units and a degree of calm returned to the city and neighbouring districts. Elsewhere in Iraq the insurgency continued and even intensified, with repeated bombings, attacks on US and Iraqi units and multiple kidnappings.[1] By the end of the month, substantial parts of Baghdad as well as Fallujah and a number of other towns and cities were effectively under the control of insurgents.[2]

The early part of September was marked by the tragic end to the siege of a school in Beslan, the return of suicide bombings in Israel, and further violence in Afghanistan, all of this in addition to the endemic problems in Iraq itself. While most of these instances of violence appeared to have little effect on the US presidential election campaign, at the end of the month some impact was felt, although this seemed unlikely to damage President Bush's prospects sufficiently to hinder his re-election.

Russia and Israel

The response of the Putin government to the Beslan school siege was to seek international support for the view that the Chechen rebellion should be seen as part of the war on terror, while rejecting international criticism of any hardline actions that the Russian authorities might take in response. Although there was little independent evidence, Russian government sources claimed that some of those taking over the school were Islamic radicals from other countries. There was broad acceptance within the Bush administration that Chechnya could be seen in this wider context, but European Union sources took a different view, questioning Russian responses much to the annoyance of the Russian authorities.

Israel, too, has worked intently to portray the Palestinian uprising as part of its own war on terror, and Israeli government representatives repeated this view following a new wave of suicide bombings early in September, the first major incidents for several months. Here again the Bush administration was sympathetic, indeed far more so than in relation to the Russian/Chechen conflict, and here again, the most common view from European Union sources was to parallel condemnation of the suicide bombings with criticism of aspects of Israeli policies. This was directed especially at the further building of settlements and the use of considerable force in Gaza.

In both cases, though, the hardline Russian and Israeli attitudes were seen across much of the Arab world as further evidence of western attempts to exert control over the Islamic world. Throughout the month, as in many previous months, there was detailed reporting of civilian casualties in the occupied territories, and the extent of the earlier destruction by Russian forces in Chechnya was well known. In such a way, there was a clear portrayal of a religion and culture under siege, even before the continuing violence in Iraq was factored in.

Afghanistan and Pakistan

In Afghanistan, some progress has been made towards holding presidential elections, but this is against a pattern of insecurity stemming from two separate factors. One is the continuing power of warlords in many parts of the country, in spite of the efforts of the Karzai administration to bring some areas of warlord control under central government authority. The other is the continuing low-level insurgency in parts of eastern and southern Afghanistan as a result of a resurgence of Taliban activity.

The International Security Assistance Force has aided the Afghan authorities in maintaining a degree of control in Kabul and in some other cities and some major transport routes, but even the current expansion takes it to less than 10,000 troops, barely a third of what is believed by independent analysts to be required. ISAF is now effectively a NATO operation, yet NATO has had difficulty in getting member states to provide the necessary forces.[3]

Even in areas away from the Taliban-inspired insurgency, there are persistent attacks on government forces and foreign security personnel. At the end of August, the Kabul offices of a US security company, DynCorp, were bombed killing seven people, and within four days during September there was an assassination attempt on Vice President Nematullah Shahrani and a suspected attempt against President Karzai himself.

There have also been further violent incidents between US forces and Taliban units. The counter-insurgency force in Afghanistan now numbers close to 20,000, the great majority being drawn from the US armed forces. This strong military presence comes nearly three years after the start of the war in Afghanistan, whereas the original expectation had been a rapid withdrawal of US forces by late 2002, with the main presence being reduced to relatively small forces located at the Bagram and Kandahar bases. Although on a smaller scale than Iraq, the end result is that US forces seem likely to be involved in combat in Afghanistan for an indefinite period.

In this context, the security situation in Pakistan remains a key factor in the region. President Musharraf has deployed Pakistani Army units in the border regions close to Afghanistan for much of the year. They have succeeded in countering some militias operating across the border but the successes, from Washington's perspective, have been limited. Musharraf therefore remains under pressure from the USA, but many of the radical groups that support anti-American actions in Afghanistan are broadly allied to those groups that continue to put pressure on Indian forces in disputed Kashmir.

Moreover, anti-American sentiments remain high in much of Pakistan and there have been recent assassination attempts against an army general and the Prime Minister designate. At the same time, the Congress Party's victory in the Indian general election means that there is greater scope for negotiations over

Kashmir and this allows the Musharraf administration a certain breathing space. It is even possible that a sustained easing of the tensions with India could strengthen Musharraf's position against radical elements in Pakistan itself.

The problem, though, is that such elements are fully aware of this and may make serious attempts to destabilise the government, most likely through further assassination attempts. One key factor here is the impact of US military actions in Iraq and of Israeli military actions in Gaza. In both cases, the continual civilian deaths and injuries are being widely reported across the region, producing difficulties for Musharraf and other pro-western governments that appear entirely unrecognised in Washington.

Insurgency and Counteraction in Iraq

Eighteen months into the Iraq war is an appropriate time to reflect on original intentions and outcomes. When the USA led a coalition to terminate the Saddam Hussein regime last year, there was an expectation that this could form the centrepiece of a Greater Middle East Initiative that would ensure the security of Gulf oil supplies and, separately, of the State of Israel. It was expected that the regime would fall quickly and that coalition forces would be widely welcomed as liberators. Within a few months it would be possible to withdraw most of the military forces and to oversee the development of a client government that would be friendly to US interests.

A key part of the plan would be the building of a number of permanent military bases, some of them with strategic locations close to the main northern and southern oilfields but with another base positioned to ensure the security of new oilfields that might be developed in the western desert region of Iraq. In parallel with this, Iraq would develop as a vigorous free market economy with a minimum of constraints and regulations, and with its plentiful oil resources forming a base for western investment.

The end result would be a pro-western free market Iraq with a continuing US military presence. In such circumstances, Iran's position would be made more difficult, with US naval forces present in the Persian Gulf and the Arabian Sea and land and air forces based in Iraq and in western Gulf states such as Kuwait and Qatar. Saudi Arabia would become less significant in geopolitical terms, in spite of its massive oil reserves, and any future instability there would be of less importance, given US influence in Iraq.

In the past eighteen months this vision has been very largely lost. The rapid move to a free market has resulted in continuing unemployment and marginalisation for millions of Iraqis, helping to fuel the insurgency, and the political transition is proving deeply problematic. Most important of all, a full-scale insurgency has evolved that is severely stretching US forces and killing hundreds of Iraqis each month.[4] The permanent US bases are certainly being built but the prospects for a stable pro-western Iraq are minimal. Instead, there is little prospect of withdrawing the occupying forces, and US military planners see the need for well over 100,000 troops to remain in Iraq for some years. More generally, anti-Americanism has increased markedly across the Arab world and beyond, with this aiding recruitment into al-Qaeda and its affiliated groups.

If the original plan for Iraq is therefore defunct, is it possible to discern the current strategy and, if so, are there further choices in the event of failure? For the present, it is fair to say that the USA is pursuing a counter-insurgency war while trying to minimise its own casualties. At the same time, it is seeking to increase the availability of Iraqi police, paramilitary and military forces as rapidly as possible. The anticipated free market is scarcely emerging, given that many of the reconstruction programmes remain at a standstill. Even so, there appears to be a hope that the insurgency can be controlled sufficiently to allow some elections in January and that, eventually, a degree of stability will be achieved.

In the short term of the next three months, US forces will continue to use their advantages in firepower to damage insurgent forces in cities such as Ramadi, Samarra and Fallujah, but there is little evidence that these actions are having an impact on the insurgency.[5] In September, eighty-one US soldiers were killed, one of the worst casualty rates since the war started, and US forces are currently experiencing over eighty attacks a day. Meanwhile, the large numbers of civilian casualties are further stimulating opposition to the US occupation, with the Alawi regime also unpopular in that it is seen as collaborating with a foreign occupying force.

The experience to date in Iraq is that responding to the problems of insurgency with substantial military force is consistently counterproductive. Such methods were tried in the summer months of 2003 and again later in the year, and they were repeated on a larger scale in April of this year. On each occasion the insurgency intensified, and it is highly likely that this will be the result of the current operations in Samarra, Fallujah, Sadr City and elsewhere. The implications are that the insurgency may not be controllable using the methods and tactics currently available to the USA.

Is there a further option that could be developed? From the little evidence currently available, an escalating and uncontrollable insurgency could lead to one of two choices for the USA. The first would be to withdraw entirely, but this would be politically unthinkable, at least for the Bush administration, given the importance of Iraq and its oil resources to current US policy in the Middle East. The second would be to withdraw almost entirely from the centres of population, falling back on the permanent bases being established close to the major oilfields. Even such a limited development would have been unthinkable a few months ago, but circumstances in Iraq do now make it a possible outcome.

Even then, though, the end result would be a substantial US military presence in key parts of Iraq. It might minimise US casualties while allowing considerable influence to be maintained in Iraq, but it would, in due course, act as a magnet for paramilitaries, including those linked to al-Qaeda, in their opposition to the US presence in the region.

Iran

While the USA is hugely preoccupied in Iraq, US-Iran relations remain deeply problematic. Iran is now reluctant to open up its nuclear facilities to IAEA inspection at the level required by the USA, and this is fuelling suspicions in Washington that a nascent nuclear weapons programme is being established. Recent reports from within Iran indicate that a new class of ballistic missiles is being developed and possibly deployed that could have a range to cover much of the region.

From an Iranian perspective, with US forces on three sides of its territory, some kind of deterrent force may be a major aspect of its current security policy, but the effect in Washington is to increase pressure for pre-emptive action, even at a time of intense commitments in Iraq. In such circumstances, such pre-emptive action, involving conventional air attacks on Iranian nuclear facilities, could come much earlier than many analysts expect. It could even happen before the US presidential election.

Chapter 7
Iraq, al-Qaeda and a Renewed Caliphate
October 2004

The Iraq Insurgency

During the course of October, the insurgency in Iraq was maintained at a high level, with scores of attacks each day on US troops and also on Iraqi government facilities and security forces.[1] The police and new Iraqi defence forces experienced particularly high numbers of casualties, but there was persistent and strong use of force by US troops and strike aircraft, with the city of Fallujah bombed repeatedly during the month.

At different times, US forces attempted to control insurgents in the cities of Ramadi and Samarra, with systematic attacks in Samarra giving rise to claims that the city had been returned fully to Iraqi government control.[2] In practice, such control was short-lived, with a resurgence of paramilitary activity during the course of the month. Even so, towards the end of October, there were indications that US military planners were putting together a large force of Marines to engage in a major assault on Fallujah.

This was considered to be the key city for the insurgency and the presumption was that if resistance in Fallujah could be overcome, then the insurgency would be hindered sufficiently for elections to go ahead in January.

Apparently because of a shortage of combat troops, the US requested British military support in areas close to Baghdad, the effect of this being to link British forces closely, if indirectly, to the anticipated attack on Fallujah.[3]

The plans for an assault on Fallujah were developed in the context of substantial further US casualties during October.[4] During the month, another sixty-five US troops were killed, bringing the figure for the three months to the end of October to 211. One key aspect of this is that these deaths come in an insurgency that has been developing for eighteen months. During that time, the US military has greatly increased the levels of protection available to its troops. Tactics and equipment have undergone radical changes and there have been persistent efforts to utilise the experience of the Israeli Defense Forces in the occupied territories.

Moreover, the US forces are all too ready to use substantial firepower, and many of the troops are now experienced in urban guerrilla warfare, being into their second term of deployment in Iraq. In spite of all this, the casualty levels remain high, giving some indication of the problems now being faced in Iraq at a time when there are deep suspicions that insurgents have successfully infiltrated elements of the new Iraqi security forces.

Casualties of War

Towards the end of October new information emerged relating to the level of civilian casualties in Iraq since the war started, and this may now throw light on the underlying reasons for the persistence, and indeed the intensification, of the insurgency.

A feature of the coalition operations throughout the first eighteen months of the Iraq war has been the deep reluctance to give any estimates of civilian casualties – as General Franks put it, 'We don't do body counts.' Instead, it has been left to non-governmental organisations such as Iraq Body Count (IBC) together with the partial release of information from the Iraq Ministry of Health, to give some indication of the human costs of the war.

IBC has provided detailed and very careful estimates of civilian deaths and injuries, using multiple press sources to verify each record of casualties. It has recorded around 15,000 deaths since the onset of the war in March 2003, with at least one third of those deaths being caused since the termination of the Saddam Hussein regime.[5]

Separate assessments from the Iraqi Ministry of Health were published during the middle part of 2004, and these confirmed a continuing cost to civilians as the insurgency developed. In the twenty-two weeks to 6 September, they recorded 3,040 Iraqis killed, and a separate *New York Times* estimate for the week up to 17 October, gained from multiple sources including hospital and mortuary sources, was of 208 Iraqis killed. The Ministry of Health and the *New York Times* figures would seem to point to an annual loss of life of over 7,000 civilians, and, on the basis of experience in other conflicts, this would mean up to 20,000 people injured.

At the end of October, and just before the US presidential election, estimates from an entirely new source suggested that the civilian death toll in Iraq might be very much higher than has previously been realised. In a detailed and peer-reviewed paper in the medical journal *The Lancet*, it was concluded that the civilian death toll may be as high as 100,000.[6]

The work was carried out by a team of public health specialists at a leading US university, Johns Hopkins, in Baltimore, working with Iraqi doctors and other medical specialists. Operating under difficult and sometimes dangerous conditions, teams of researchers interviewed substantial numbers of Iraqis from numerous sites across Iraq designed to be as representative as possible. Using sample sizes very much larger than opinion polling, they were able to determine that the risk of violent death has risen more than fifty-fold since the start of the occupation and infant mortality has almost doubled.

Some of the increases in death rates have been due to weakened medical facilities, transport difficulties and wide-ranging disruptions, but much of the greatly increased death rate was directly due to coalition military actions. Furthermore, many of the extrapolations were done in a conservative manner – the results for Fallujah, for example, were not included because of the specifically high death toll there resulting from the coalition offensive last April.

The authors of the paper do not specifically claim a civilian death toll of 100,000; they say that it is a reasonable assessment based on their extensive work. If only remotely accurate, it suggests that coalition air and ground attacks have had a much greater impact on civilian populations than has previously been realised. At the very least, the paper supports the idea that other estimates based directly on individually recorded and published deaths may be markedly conservative in their results.

Even if an assumption is made that the *Lancet* paper is overestimating the casualties, and that they are closer to other figures of around 15,000, this still means a loss of life and of serious injury affecting close to 50,000 people, which in turn represents about one in 500 of the entire Iraqi population. This suggests that a very large proportion, perhaps even a majority of the entire population of the country, is likely to have had family or neighbourhood experience of death or serious injury due to coalition action. If the Johns Hopkins study is even remotely accurate, the impact is very much higher. This would, at the very least, help explain the developing opposition to the coalition forces and the increasing perception of them as occupiers. It would also explain the widespread reality of tacit if not open support for the insurgency.

It further follows that if the USA and its coalition partners actually increase the intensity of attacks on cities such as Fallujah, Ramadi and Samarra, as well as parts of Baghdad itself, then the increased civilian casualties that will result will be likely to further intensify opposition to the coalition.

The bin Laden Video

Another substantial development at the end of the October, just days before the US presidential election, was the release of a videotape of the al-Qaeda leader, Osama bin Laden.[7] At first sight, this may simply be seen as an attempt to influence the US election, presumably to aid George Bush in his re-election contest. Even though bin Laden might well prefer a Bush second term, not least because a Christian fundamentalist in the White House helps him in the short term, it is unlikely that this was the main reason. Instead, the message is more probably directed at four linked audiences outside the USA, with the timing, style and content all relevant to achieving certain aims.

In terms of timing, four days before the US election could hardly be better, ensuring that the tape received prime-time coverage around the world. Moreover, with so much attention on the US election, releasing this tape at such a time ensured that it remained in the media for several days rather than receding within a few hours.

The style of the message is different to earlier examples in the sense that it presents bin Laden as a figure seeking to exude authority. The lectern, the dress and the style all serve to present the image of a figurehead – not a military leader but more someone who is developing a long-term international role, even if he himself does not survive much longer. In part, this latest message may be intended for posterity.

As to the message, its most significant aspect is the reference to Lebanon and 1982. In June of that year, the Israeli defence minister, Ariel Sharon, launched Operation 'Peace for Galilee'. The stated aim was to eliminate the capacity of Palestinian militias to launch short-range unguided Katyusha rockets at targets in Galilee, but the real aim was to occupy most of Southern Lebanon up to Beirut, destroying the PLO leadership then entrenched in the western part of the city, and countering the Syrian presence in much of central Lebanon.

The well-equipped Israeli forces reached Beirut but faced much stronger opposition from Palestinian militia, resulting in a bitter siege of West Beirut that lasted many weeks. Israeli artillery and strike aircraft used repeated bombardments to attempt to dislodge the militia, with close to 20,000 people dying during the siege, at least half of them civilians.

Later that year, Israeli military forces allowed Lebanese Christian Phalange militia to massacre Palestinians in the Sabra and Shatila refugee camps. This increased the existing bitter divisions in Israeli society over the purpose and conduct of the war, and resulted in the temporary demotion of Sharon. More generally, though, the Israeli Defense Forces found it impossible to maintain control of Southern Lebanon in the face of increasing Hezbollah militia activity and withdrew from most of the territory by 1985.

Bin Laden's reference to Lebanon recalls for Arab audiences the repeated Israeli attacks on West Beirut's high-rise blocks of apartments, the 'towers', and it also reminds many of them of the subsequent 'defeat' of Israeli military forces and of Sharon's role in the entire operation. Moreover, the Israeli operation in 1982 was presumed across much of the Middle East to have had US backing – the USA was one of the states subsequently putting in peace-enforcing troops, was responsible for actions against radical Lebanese militia, including the shelling of towns and villages, and suffered a huge loss in the killing of 241 US Marines in a suicide bomb attack at Beirut Airport in October 1983.

Bin Laden therefore puts together the claim for US involvement in Israeli expansion into Lebanon, Israeli attacks on 'Arab towers' and the role of Ariel Sharon, but also the withdrawal of the Israelis from much of Lebanon and of the USA from that same country. It is a message designed to appeal to Palestinians and to the Shi'a communities with their links to Hezbollah, both communities that have offered less than full support for al-Qaeda.

In addition, two more general audiences are the focus for the message. One is the convinced supporters of al-Qaeda and its many associates – for them the message is that Osama bin Laden is still there, and can claim to be a figure of increased authority. The other is for a much wider Arab and Islamic audience and

71

demonstrates that he has the power to dominate the world's media and have a direct impact on the election of the President of the world's most powerful state.

Iraq and a New Caliphate

Bin Laden's concentration on Israel and the USA and their activities in Lebanon in 1982 and his claim that these actions were his original motivation is almost certainly an exercise in hindsight. It is chosen now to remind his audience that, in his analysis, the early 1980s represented a period in which Islam was clearly under attack from a combination of the USA and Israel, just as he will now justify al-Qaeda and its affiliates because of Israel's hardline control of the Palestinians and of American involvement in Iraq.

It is here that the casualty levels connect. In Iraq, many thousands of civilians have been killed, with hundreds dying every month. While this is happening, Israel is using persistent and massive force to control the Palestinian *intifada*. According to the Israeli newspaper, *Haaretz*, 159 Palestinians were killed in the Gaza Strip in October, with fifty of them civilians including children.

Osama bin Laden's attempts to embrace the Palestinian cause may be relatively recent, and certainly undesired by most Palestinians, but he has sought to make this one of his three short-term aims, along with the dissolution of the House of Saud as the unacceptably corrupt Keeper of the Two Holy Places, and the expulsion of western forces from the Middle East.

It is the long-term aim of bin Laden and al-Qaeda that is actually more significant and has a particular relevance to Iraq. Bin Laden and his associates have consistently denigrated the elitism and wealth of existing regimes across the Middle East, just as he denigrates the perceived elites in the USA. In his recent video, he describes the USA as 'similar to regimes in our countries, half of which are governed by the military and the other half of which are governed by the sons of kings and presidents; and we have long experience with them'. He continues: 'In both categories, you find many who are characterised by hubris, arrogance, greed, and unlawful acquisition of money.'[8]

For the al-Qaeda leadership, there is the long-term aim of destroying such regimes, initially in the Islamic world, and replacing them with acceptable 'pure' Islamic governance. What form this would take, and whether it would relate to current state boundaries is less than clear, but there is a sense of the need to re-establish a caliphate in the Middle East, perhaps as a prelude to a wider process of conversion across the world.

Over 1,400 years there have been periods of notable caliphates, although many were of more symbolic importance than their actual power at the time. Even the longest-lasting caliphate, the Abbasids, which lasted for 500 years from 749 CE, involved long periods of Turkish, Persian or other rule. Two things, though, make the Abbasid Caliphate significant in the current era. One is that it certainly coincided with the most notable period of Arab civilisation, including the flowering of mathematics, the sciences, the arts and architecture, mostly at a time when Western Europe was barely struggling out of the Dark Ages and long before the colonisation of North America.

The second factor is that for most of those five centuries, the Abbasid Caliphate was centred on what was then the hugely important city of Baghdad. This is now seen to be occupied by western forces, and can so easily be represented as a Christian/Zionist axis of control in the heart of the Islamic world.

Much of this may be perception and much of it may be symbolism. Moreover, al-Qaeda and its associates had virtually no connections with the largely secular Saddam Hussein prior to last year, even if he did seek to embrace Islam at the end of his rule. Until a little over a year ago, the al-Qaeda group was far more concerned with Saudi Arabia, Afghanistan, Pakistan and other Islamic countries across the world. Iraq was scarcely on the radar until the Bush administration began the operation to terminate the regime and bring Iraq into the western fold.

Analysts currently speak of the value to al-Qaeda of the US occupation of Iraq.[9] It provides the insurgents and foreign paramilitaries in Iraq with well over 100,000 'targets' – in a real sense America has come to them. But the value goes far beyond that. What the occupation of Iraq is beginning to do is to provide al-Qaeda and bin Laden with a whole new focus on what they may well have expected to be many decades of conflict to 'purify' Islam.[10]

For them, the foreign occupation of Iraq, the seat of the most distinguished caliphate in early Islamic history, is an unexpected but quite remarkable bonus. It is one that they may see playing to their advantage, not just in the coming months or years but over a decade or more, an aspect of the occupation of Iraq that is almost entirely unrecognised in London, let alone Washington.[11]

Chapter 8
Fallujah and
its Aftermath
November 2004

Towards the end of October, there were numerous reports of a substantial build-up of US troops in the region to the west of Baghdad. All the indications pointed to a major assault on insurgent positions in the city of Fallujah, with some suggestions that the final decision would depend on the outcome of the US presidential election on 2 November. The assumption was that if George W. Bush were re-elected, there would be an immediate decision to go ahead with the assault on the basis that this would result in a severe setback for the insurgency and would do much to ensure that elections could take place in Iraq at the end of January.[1]

In the event, President Bush was re-elected, the assault went ahead and, some four weeks later, there are abundant indications that the insurgency continues to develop. This is not, however, the perception among some of the more right-wing commentators in Washington, where the analysis points to a developing success for US forces in Iraq. Which viewpoint turns out to be correct will provide the clearest indication of prospects for decreased violence and increased security in Iraq in the coming months.

The Election Outcome

Although there have been persistent reports of electoral problems in some US states, most notably Ohio, there is a general acceptance that President Bush has won a second term by a reasonably clear majority in the electoral college, backed up by an overall majority of the votes cast. Moreover, the Republican Party has consolidated its control of both Houses of Congress, giving President Bush a particularly strong power base for his second term.

The Cabinet appointments made so far indicate a move to the right, especially in the area of foreign and security policy, with Colin Powell replaced at the State Department by Condoleezza Rice. Perhaps more significant have been the many changes and resignations at the Central Intelligence Agency, where there is now a clear presumption that CIA activities must be more clearly moulded to the needs of the second Bush administration.

Although the mood in Republican circles is buoyant, the issue of Iraq remains central to the problem of extending the idea of the New American Century. This world-view presupposes that it is possible to pre-empt the dangerous activities of rogue states such as Iraq, Iran and North Korea, and that the methods being used to pursue the war on terror are proving effective.

The problem is that al-Qaeda and its associates remain highly active, as shown by October's attacks on the Australian Embassy in Djakarta and the Taba Hilton in Sinai.[2] Meanwhile, Iraq remains deeply enmeshed in insurgency. This is probably the central reason why the overthrow of insurgents in Fallujah was seen as so important. With the Bush administration safely returned to power, potential civilian casualties would be less of a concern and the taking of Fallujah could therefore more easily involve the use of heavy military force.

Fallujah was seen as important because there was a firm belief that the city was acting as the primary centre of the entire insurgency throughout central and northern Iraq. By having a major urban centre that was effectively a 'no go' area for US and Iraqi security forces, insurgents could train, organise, produce car bombs and other weapons and use Fallujah as a staging post for widespread operations.

Immediately after the main assault, Professor Mackubin Thomas Owens of the Naval War College, wrote an analysis for the *Weekly Standard* (6 December) in Washington, arguing that the taking of the city had been a major military success but that it had to be extended to all the other centres of population that were largely or partially controlled by insurgents. In his view:

> All wars hinge on logistics. No force, conventional or guerrilla, can continue to fight if it is not resupplied. Storming Fallujah was absolutely essential to the destruction of the rebel logistics infrastructure.[3]

While few military analysts would dispute this view, the real question that arises from this assessment is whether the insurgency in Iraq does need to maintain a relatively small number of major logistics centres, or whether it is already much more dispersed and integrated throughout many of the Sunni communities of Iraq. If it is the latter, then the insurgency will be extremely difficult to control, and meaningful elections in January will be impossible.

The Fallujah Assault

Four days into the military operation in Fallujah, the *International Herald Tribune* reported (11 November) that 'American forces cornered insurgents in a small section of Fallujah after a stunningly swift advance in which they seized control of 70 percent of the military stronghold.' The use of substantial military force, including tanks, artillery, assault helicopters, strike aircraft and the highly destructive AC-130 gunship, all enabled Marines and Army troops to take over much of the city, albeit while causing massive structural damage and civilian casualties.

Within ten days, the assault was being represented in the USA as a substantial military success, a view made easier by the copious embedding of reporters with US troops in contrast to an almost total absence of reporting from within the city. Even so, three separate issues emerged during the latter part of November that cast serious doubt on the 'success' of the operation.

The first is that there was a substantial increase in attacks on US and Iraqi security forces elsewhere in the country at the very time the Fallujah operation was under way.[4] During the course of October, there had typically been sixty to seventy insurgent attacks a day, but this rose to around 120 a day in mid-November, returning to the previous level towards the end of the month. Moreover, there was a substantial increase in major insurgent operations in cities such as Ramadi and Mosul, with insurgents taking over large parts of the latter city. The situation there became so serious that the US military had to divert several thousand troops from elsewhere in Iraq in an attempt to restore control.[5]

The second issue relates to the assumption, prior to the attack on Fallujah, that the city was the primary location for 5,000 or more insurgents. During the military operations in the city, it became apparent that there were far fewer insurgents, possibly around 2,000–3,000, with many of them having left the city before the assault began. Even so, insurgent casualties were high, with almost certainly well over 1,000 killed, but this, in turn, has to be put in the context that there were still persistent attacks on US forces in the city by the end of November. In other words, it did not prove possible to fully secure the city, despite a well-equipped force of close to 15,000 US and Iraqi troops facing a much smaller number of insurgents armed only with light weapons.

The third issue relates to US casualties. During the month of November, 136 soldiers were killed, the highest number in any month since the war began in March of last year. Furthermore, the number of injuries was particularly high. Taking the period from 4 November to 30 November, US forces experienced 1,265 casualties, with almost half of them sufficiently badly wounded to require airlifting to Landstuhl military hospital in Germany and then on to the USA. Because of the use of body armour, and the high standards of battlefield casualty support available, many of those wounded survived, whereas in other conflicts they would have died. The other side of this is that many of them have sustained very serious injuries that will affect them for life.

The Fallujah Aftermath

During the Fallujah operation, there was worldwide press coverage of the conflict, with intense reporting from within the US military. As the fighting progressed, more information became available concerning the damage being done to the city and the increasing numbers of civilian casualties. Although no reliable figures are yet available, it is probable that they number in the thousands.

After the end of the main assault, many of the western media reporters were withdrawn from Iraq, and those that remained were largely based in very secure areas in Baghdad, with the security situation making travel around the country virtually impossible. As a result, news of the continuing insurgency comes largely from a small number of Iraqi journalists working for agencies, together with information on some blog sites.

This situation is resulting in two quite separate views of the war in Iraq for two very different audiences. In the USA, there is an impression of success, with Fallujah now in US hands, an election in prospect, and little news seeping through of the level of the insurgency in the rest of the country.[6]

Across the Middle East, however, the reporting is entirely different. The vivid TV images from reporters embedded with US units of heavy weaponry being used against mosques, houses and shops in Fallujah, have been supplemented with increasing numbers of reports of civilian casualties and the plight of refugees. This has been coupled with graphic accounts of the levels of destruction wrought on the city by what is seen throughout most of the region as an occupying force, bent on destroying the 'city of mosques'.

Which of these views is the more accurate, and what are the implications of recent developments? Supporters of the current US strategy insist that the operation in Fallujah was essential to control the insurgency, and that similar operations, with substantial use of firepower, are going to be necessary throughout much of central Iraq. The view is that Fallujah was a turning point and that this, and other similar operations, will mark the beginning of the end of the insurgency.

If this is the case, then we would expect a substantial degree of optimism among military analysts. This should be coupled with the likelihood of reasonably early withdrawals of US forces as the insurgency begins to decay, now that it is being deprived of its key centres of operations such as Fallujah

The evidence so far suggests otherwise. Indeed, at the end of November it was confirmed that US forces in Iraq are to be increased from the current level of 138,000 to 150,000. What is more significant is that all of the additional troops are front-line combat troops, including two battalions of paratroops from the 82nd Airborne Division. Given that only about half of the US forces currently in Iraq are front-line troops, this is a substantial increase, especially as the initial deployment of the 82nd Airborne troops, who currently serve as the US Army's rapid deployment emergency reserve, is to be for four months.[7]

This substantial reinforcement has to be seen in context in two quite different ways. One is that it is a clear indication that substantial efforts to create a viable Iraqi army, backed up by a renewed police force, are proving deeply problematic. The Iraqi police, in particular, are taking serious casualties on an almost daily basis. Meanwhile, very few of the new army units are considered to be reliable partners for the US forces, and informed analysts consider it will take five to ten years to build up a force sufficient to control the country.

The second factor is the contrast between what is now happening and what was originally anticipated. At the start of the war last year, it was confidently expected that US troop deployments in Iraq would have been reduced to about 50,000 by the end of 2003. While the majority might be withdrawn within a year or so, a much smaller number would remain in the country on a long-term basis at the small number of permanent bases being established.

By the end of last year that plan was in disarray, and the revised plan was that there could be slow withdrawals of troops during 2004. The numbers did actually drop to about 110,000 last February, but they had to be increased substantially as the insurgency developed during the spring, with close to 30,000 troops added in the following months. Now we have a further increase, with the entire trend echoing the previously derided views of Army Chief of Staff General Eric Shinseki, expressed before the invasion, that several hundred thousand troops would be required to occupy the country.

The insurgency in Iraq is therefore deeply embedded and showing every sign of persisting if not intensifying, in spite of the assault on its supposed centre in Fallujah.[8] Even so, with President Bush firmly ensconced for a second term, it will be entirely unacceptable for his administration to have Iraq as a major ongoing problem, so we should expect to see the continued use of substantial military force throughout the towns and cities of central and northern Iraq. On past experience, this will lead to a further increase in anti-Americanism within the country that will, in turn aid the insurgency.

Furthermore, the impact of Fallujah and the future US military operations in Iraq will continue to be widely reported across the wider Arab and Islamic world. The effects of this are likely to be cumulative, and should be expected to lead to further support for the insurgency in Iraq and for the wider activities of al-Qaeda and its associates. It therefore looks as if Fallujah, far from being a turning point for the US efforts to control the insurgency, will be one further part of a conflict that is still in its early stages.

Chapter 9
Towards a Third Year of War
December 2004

In the immediate aftermath of the US assault on the city of Fallujah in early November, there was a belief in many Republican circles in Washington that the assault was being successful in destroying perhaps the key centre of opposition to the US military presence in Iraq. The result would be a curbing of the entire insurgency, enabling elections to proceed with little hindrance at the end of January.

In analysing the events of that month, the previous briefing in this series (Chapter 8) suggested that the contrast between those who took such a view and others who saw little change, would provide 'the clearest indication of prospects for decreased violence and increased security in Iraq in the coming months'.

Elections and Insurgency
A month later, the early indications are that the insurgency is continuing and may even be deepening.[1] This is not to say that

the elections will not take place – they almost certainly will – but that they may make little difference to the levels of insecurity across much of the country.

In a sense, the elections will be just one further marker in a long-term pattern in which particular events have been expected to lead to improvements. The original occupation of Iraq in April 2003 was expected to be a process of liberation, but an insurgency began to develop within days of the termination of the Saddam Hussein regime. Three months later, the killing of Uday and Qusay Hussein in Mosul was expected to severely limit opposition, yet the following months saw a further escalation of violence, not least with the attacks on the UN and Red Cross buildings in Baghdad.[2]

Towards the end of the year, US military sources were saying that the insurgency was essentially controlled by a handful of extended families, that they had been identified and were being watched and that their activities would be progressively controlled.

Then, in December, Saddam Hussein was himself captured amid scenes of confident expectations of the insurgency's demise. Once again, this view was proved wrong, with April 2004 being one of the most violent months since the war began.

Even so, the handover of power to the Alawi regime at the end of June was expected to undermine the opposition to US occupation, but this, too, proved illusory, leading to widespread violence in August that included protracted fighting in Najaf. Meanwhile hundreds of Iraqi civilians were being killed each month, and the insurgents themselves placed increased emphasis on targeting Iraqi police and national guard units as well as US military units and civilian contractors. It was in this context that, towards the end of the year, the assault on Fallujah was both prepared and implemented.

US Casualties

Close to two months after the start of the assault on the city, a tentative analysis can be made of its effects. The first point to make is that the last six months of 2004 was the worst such period for US casualties since the war began. The number of soldiers killed through combat or non-combat injuries was 503, compared with 401 in the first six months of the year. This may be explained, in part, by the increased intensity of US military action, especially in Fallujah but, the month after that assault, December, saw seventy-five US soldiers killed, one of the highest monthly casualty rates since the start of the war.

In some parts of the country, US military sources reported a decrease in the rate of attacks during December, down to about sixty a day compared with a rate of well over 100 during November. At the same time, three trends were indicative of the changing nature of the insurgency. One was a further increase in the use of suicide bombings, a form of insurgency that is very difficult to counter, and a second was the increased number of attacks against Iraqi units, with perhaps less attention given to the heavily protected and well-armed US forces.

The third trend, though, was towards better intelligence being available to the insurgents. This was demonstrated most powerfully by the attack on a US base near Mosul on 21 December, where insurgents penetrated the mess tent used by US soldiers and contractors, detonating a bomb with devastating effect. Fifteen US troops were among those killed, and the attack caused considerable concern among US forces across Iraq.[3]

Insurgent Capabilities

While there may be strong support for elections in the Kurdish north-east of Iraq and in many of the largely Shi'a areas, it is also clear that the insurgency is deeply embedded in much of the country and is certainly not limited to the so-called 'Sunni triangle' north of Baghdad. Where US forces stage major operations in cities such as Fallujah, Ramadi and Samarra, there may be a temporary decrease in insurgent activity there, but in some of the areas of operation the insurgents regroup and become active once more, or else they move their operations elsewhere. This was most apparent in the immediate aftermath of the Fallujah assault where there was a sudden burst of insurgent activity in Mosul, resulting in most of the Iraqi police force leaving their posts in the face of persistent attacks.

Perhaps the most remarkable indication of the intensity of the insurgency came in an assessment from the head of the Iraqi intelligence service within the Alawi regime, General Shahwani, right at the end of 2004. He assessed the total strength of the insurgency at around 40,000 active paramilitaries backed by up to 160,000 active supporters willing to provide intelligence, shelter and logistics support and even engage, on occasions in attacks.

This contrasts with US estimates given in October of 5,000 to 20,000 full-time or part-time insurgents, but Shahwani's figures were not immediately countered by US sources. It is in even sharper contrast to the belief, expressed a year earlier, that the insurgency was limited to those few extended families – 'remnants' of the old regime.

Other evidence of the depth of the security problem comes from recently released figures for the number of people being held in detention by US and British forces. Although Iraq is theoretically under the control of the government of Iyad Alawi, there has been virtually no decrease in the number of detainees held by occupation forces. These are currently held in three major locations, Abu Ghraib near Baghdad, Camp Bucca near the Kuwait border and the British-controlled Al-Shuaiba base near Basra. Close to 10,000 people are in detention, and almost all are there because of suspected participation in the insurgency.

Of this total, only 350 are foreigners. It is possible that some foreign detainees have been removed to other locations in the Gulf region or even further away, but these figures do support the information available from other sources that only about one in twenty of all the insurgents are non-Iraqis. Moreover, the foreign paramilitaries active in Iraq do not seem to come especially from either of the two countries that US sources claim to be undermining Iraqi security – Iran and Syria. There are currently reported to be only twenty-two Iranians in detention, and the Syrians being held are outnumbered by nationals of Egypt and Saudi Arabia.

Counterinsurgency Experience

Although the parallels are far from appropriate in every sense, in terms of counter-insurgency operations it is instructive to compare the current situation in Iraq with other examples. In conventional military operations, it is usually considered necessary for attackers to outnumber defenders by a ratio of about 3:1. This is not always the case and is dependent on many other issues, not least the extent of defence support and the military capabilities of both sides.

In insurgency and counter-insurgency operations, it is often the case that a ratio of 10:1 is considered necessary in order to suppress an insurgency. Northern Ireland in the 1970s was a complex insurgency in an even more complex political environment, but it is worth recalling that the total paramilitary strength of the Provisional IRA was never more than a few hundred, albeit supported by many thousands more and enjoying widespread if disjointed community support. Throughout that decade, the UK Government had forces drawn from the British Army, the Royal Ulster Constabulary and other units numbering well over 20,000 – yet it was unable to control the Provisional IRA, which eventually was even able to engage in economic targeting in Britain in the early 1990s to severe political effect.

Other insurgencies may, on occasion, have other effects, but the reality is that a substantial minority of the population of central Iraq now supports the insurgents, their levels of activity are intense, and they show no signs whatsoever of any decrease in their capabilities.[4]

The Second Bush Administration

How does the security situation in Iraq relate to the formation of the second Bush administration? In Washington, that administration is now taking shape, as discussed in last month's assessment, and three features are relevant. One is the retirement of Colin Powell as Secretary of State, removing one of the relatively moderate and cautious senior figures in the administration. A second is the manner in which new figures taking on more formal cabinet roles are drawn very heavily from White House insiders. This goes well beyond Condoleezza Rice at the State Department and amounts to a consolidation in positions of authority of those most trusted by President Bush.

A third is less clear-cut at present but relates back to the neoconservative vision of a New American Century. What appears to be happening is that this movement has got a substantial new lease of life following President Bush's re-election success and, with it, a determination to consolidate its world-view in order to ensure that it survives long after George W. Bush has retired to Crawford, Texas.

Since the New American Century project is very much a matter of world vision, the main emphasis is on foreign policy and international security, and within this context the Middle East remains central. Whatever the major problems now evident in Iraq, the region retains its importance, even if that requires more radical policies than have so far been implemented. Two examples are the attitude towards Syria and the question of terrorism detainees.

Within neoconservative circles, much of the blame for the continuing problems in Iraq is being aimed at Iran and Syria.[5] Even though the evidence indicates that their actual influence in the Iraq insurgency is low level, both are being singled out for strong criticism. Action against Iran is problematic, given the more positive attitudes of European powers and the growing economic links between Iran and China, but Syria is certainly being singled out for potential pressure in the coming months, quite possibly extending even to limited military action.

On the matter of detainees, the hardline nature of the administration is illustrated by an interagency review that is now under way in Washington over the long-term future of prisoners being held at Guantánamo and elsewhere. This even goes so far as to include plans for indefinite detention that would apply to those detainees whom the administration does not want to release but is unwilling to bring to trial. These could be potentially lifetime detentions and could involve two options.

One would involve the building of a new 200-place facility, provisionally termed 'Camp 6', for long-term detention under US military authority. The other would be to house detainees in US-built prisons in their own countries, such as Yemen, Saudi Arabia or Afghanistan. In all cases, detainees would not have the status of prisoner of war and would lack legal redress.[6]

These two examples – the possibility of pre-emptive military action against Syria, and the new approach to indefinite detention without trial – are both indications of the more hardline policies now being countenanced in Washington. It is possible that both will be countered by the vigour of domestic political debate, but there is little sign of that so far. That, at least, is an early indication that the neoconservative outlook so prominent in Washington is not a passing fad but something that is far more deep-seated within the evolution of the US political system.

Chapter 10
Elections and Their Consequences
January 2005

The first month of 2005 saw the inauguration of President Bush, further developments in the formation of his second administration, the consolidation of the position of the newly elected Palestinian leader, Mahmoud Abbas, and a series of events leading up to the elections for a Transitional Assembly in Iraq.

In President Bush's inaugural address, there was a persistent emphasis on the spreading of freedom, and remarkably little mention of events in Iraq. At the same time, the Republican successes in the November elections, not least in both Houses of Congress, meant that there was a real sense of mandated purpose, with further indications that the new administration would take a particularly hard line with Iran and Syria.[1]

Although precise details of levels of turn-out in the Iraqi elections remain uncertain at the time of writing, there is substantial evidence that the intensity of voting was high in the major Shi'a and Kurdish provinces of Iraq, and slightly higher than the very low turnouts anticipated in Sunni towns and cities (see Chapter 11). At the very end of the month there was therefore a sense of vindication in Washington, with this likely to further strengthen the position of neoconservative elements in the capital. Whether this position will be sustained will largely depend on events in the next two to three months, but it is also relevant to make a careful analysis of some of the more recent trends, especially in relation to the Israeli/Palestinian confrontation, the Iraq insurgency and political developments in Washington.

Israel and Palestine: A Possibility of Progress

The clear-cut election of Mahmoud Abbas as the Palestinian leader has resulted in a more positive attitude in Washington towards a two-state solution. This, coupled with the initial ability of the Palestinian leadership to enforce some control of the more radical paramilitaries, means that there is relatively more pressure on the Sharon government to make concessions in any future negotiating process.

At a superficial level, the provisional decision to enforce the withdrawal of several thousand Jewish settlers from Gaza would seem to be a sign of good intent, as would some limited withdrawals of settlements from peripheral areas of the West Bank. In reality, both of these moves have much more to do with internal security problems than the peace process, and further progress will therefore depend more on future offers that relate specifically to potential negotiations on a lasting peace.

In Gaza, the level of opposition to Israeli occupation has been so intense that maintaining the security of the Jewish settlers has become steadily more untenable for the Israeli Defense Forces, in spite of the persistent use of considerable military force including targeted assassinations. The 7,000 settlers control a size-able minority of the land area of Gaza which otherwise has 1.2 million Palestinians, a third of them crowded into refugee camps with no prospect of returning to their original homes in Israel.

If the settlers are indeed withdrawn, future Israeli policy towards Gaza will be crucial. One possibility is that rapid economic development is enabled in the territory, with the airport reopened, port facilities developed and rapid industrialisation encouraged. Although the pattern of recent years has been for many educated young people to leave Gaza for the wider Middle East and the western world, there is a high level of education among the remaining population, and much potential for rapid development, especially if serious assistance is available from Gulf Arab states, European and American agencies and international financial institutions. Such a process, in concert with developments on the West Bank, could greatly improve the prospects of a viable Palestinian state, but will be impossible without the constructive assistance of Israel.

The other possibility is a development of the current situation in which Gaza is akin to a huge open prison. Israel controls its own extensive land borders with Gaza and the small Egyptian border. It has clear control of the limited sea routes and effectively determines the water supplies as well – a crucial commodity for Gaza. The airport remains closed. With near-total control of entry and exit, Israel has almost complete dominance of the Gaza economy, which is currently close to being moribund. In due course, the Israeli authorities may allow more movement of Palestinians into industrial areas close to the border with Gaza, either in Israel or Egypt, but they will be able to continue to maintain rigorous control of all substantive economic activity. The Israeli view is that the extreme control exerted over Gaza is essential to ensure Israel's domestic security, but the paradox is that this very control, and the levels of poverty and marginalisation within Gaza, provide a continuing recruitment incentive for Islamic paramilitaries.

If developments in Gaza are likely to give some indication of long-term Israeli intentions, then it is the complex of policies in the West Bank that is even more significant. Over the past thirty-eight years there has been widespread colonisation of many parts of the West Bank by Jewish settlers. The pace of settlement construction has varied with the political climate, but the last ten years have seen a particular expansion, backed up by a quite remarkable level of Israeli security control, made even more tough in the wake of the al-Aqsa *intifada*, which started in September 2000 following Ariel Sharon's incursion onto Haram al-Sharif (Temple Mount) in Jerusalem. There are now over 300,000 Jewish settlers in the West Bank and East Jerusalem, in a land area occupied by over two million Palestinians.

Prior to the major violence and Israeli incursions into a number of centres of Palestinian population in April 2002, there was already substantial Israeli security control of much of the West Bank, but this has since increased greatly to encompass over eighty per cent of the land area. Moreover, the distribution of settlements, the numerous strategic 'settler-only' roads that link them, and more than a hundred roadblocks on other main roads mean that Israeli control of the Palestinian population, and indeed the economic and political life of the West Bank is virtually complete.

From an Israeli perspective, it is again argued that this is all essential for Israel's internal security, not least as the impact of the suicide or martyr bombings of recent years has had a profound effect on Israeli perceptions of vulnerability. Over the past two years, the response has reached the level of building a 'wall' around much of the West Bank. The wall does not separate off the West Bank, leaving Palestinian communities to get on with their own lives, since the internal security patrols and almost all the settlements remain. What it does do, though, is to give Israelis an impression of security. From the Palestinian standpoint, though, it takes substantial areas of Palestinian land into Israel, adding to a further perception of marginalisation. This is heightened by the persistent controls of population movement within the West Bank, particularly the near impossibility of moving between the north and south of the West Bank across the area dominated by Jerusalem and its immediate environs.

What is required in the next few months is a series of major concessions from Israel. Time is short, in that Mahmoud Abbas may have a relatively brief honeymoon period, and much of the prospect for progress rests on whether the Sharon government is genuinely committed to wholesale Israeli withdrawal and the consequent development of a viable Palestinian state. Two factors may militate against this. One is that internal Israeli politics have moved decidedly towards a more hawkish stance. In part this is due to the impact of the bombings, but it also relates to the immigration into Israel of around a million people during the 1990s from the former Soviet Union and Eastern Europe. Many of these are utterly determined to achieve security and most are firm supporters of the current administration.

US Political Developments

The second factor relates to significant if largely unrecognised developments in US domestic politics. Successive US administrations have long been seen as the strongest supporters of the State of Israel, with key lobbying groups such as the America-Israel Public Affairs Committee being highly effective in maintaining this outlook, not least with considerable support from Jewish communities in the USA. In recent years, that support has tended to wane, but has been more than countered by the growing electoral significance of evangelical Christian communities that are directly committed to the survival of the State of Israel. Known most commonly as Christian Zionists, they form a large minority of the evangelical Christian churches in the USA that collectively involve over 100 million people. Moreover, they have a higher-than-average electoral commitment that is dominated by support for the Republican Party.[2]

Christian Zionism is essentially a belief that it is part of God's plan that biblical Israel should be the home of the Jews in preparation for the Second Coming that will involve an Earthly reign for a millennium, centred on Jerusalem. This dispensation theology (God giving a dispensation to the Jews) now has at its heart the survival of the modern-day State of Israel centred on Jerusalem. This core part of the Christian Zionist stance has resulted in numerous groups that are willing and able to work with the Israeli government and the Israel lobby in Washington.

More generally, Christian Zionism dovetails with many aspects of neoconservatism, but it is especially significant in relation to the foreign and security policies of the Bush administration in the Middle East. It is a near-perfect match, in that electoral support from many millions of evangelical Christians for the born-again President Bush provides a political base of real value to the administration.

There are thus two particular factors that have to be appreciated in analysing prospects for positive change in the Israel-Palestine confrontation – the changes within Israel with the influx of migrants in the 1990s, and the growing significance of Christian Zionists in the USA. Both are factors that may make moves towards an economically viable Palestinian state deeply problematic.

Iraq: Insurgency and Elections

During the early part of January, the insurgency in Iraq continued to gather strength, against the earlier predictions from Washington that the assault on Fallujah would do it irreversible damage. In the period from November to January, the coalition forces lost 345 troops, 316 of them from the USA. In January alone, US losses were 107 killed and over 500 wounded, the third worst month since the war began nearly two years ago. By the end of the month, total US losses were approaching 1,500 killed and 11,000 injured since the start of the war. During the month, the Iraqi authorities also lost scores of police and security personnel in addition to numerous assassinations of senior security officers, members of the judiciary and government officials.[3]

In the run-up to the election, American and Iraqi planners put into operation a programme to enhance security for the day of the election itself. The numerous measures included border closures, tight curfews and the banning of private vehicles from roads. US military forces conducted a series of major convoy operations prior to the election to ensure that in the electoral period itself there would be little need for the movement of vulnerable convoys. This measure also meant that the US military, already reinforced by 15,000 additional troops, could divert many of its logistics and support units to patrols and other security operations. The end result was to produce a high degree of 'close-down' in many of the more insecure parts of Iraq, although it was a tactic that could only be maintained for the duration of the electoral period.

The early indications are that the Transitional Assembly will be dominated by Shi'a political groups, with the Kurds having a significant minority. With a boycott by most Sunni-orientated parties and a low voter turn-out in central Iraq, the Sunni minority will have a minimal role in central political developments over the next year unless majority parties set out specifically, and successfully, to bring them in.

To a very large extent, the next three months will be the key period in terms of the insurgency and its contrast with possible political evolution in Iraq. It could be that the insurgency will diminish in the short term, although the US determination to maintain a long-term military presence in Iraq most likely means that there will be a persistent state of violence.[4] Even in the short term, the Pentagon is planning to maintain forces at close to current levels for the next two years, suggesting that military realities may be different from the political message of apparent progress now coming from Washington.[5]

Behind this, there remains the Washington security paradigm and the manner in which it is dominated by the neoconservative political agenda. This embraces continued strong support for Israel, the determination to retain high levels of influence in Iraq including a military presence, and a willingness to take action against other members of the 'axis of evil' most notably Syria and Iran.[6] There is no real change in this stance and, in this context, the rise of Christian Zionism could well be an additional hindrance to prospects for serious progress towards peace in the Middle East.

Chapter 11
Limitations of Power
February 2005

After the Iraq Election

In the month since the elections in Iraq, there have been two separate developments that are relevant to the analysis of possible trends over the coming months – the actual election result and the status of the insurgency. The election resulted in a legislature that will be dominated by Kurdish and Shi'a-orientated parties. As expected, electoral turnout in the Kurdish north-east of Iraq was exceptionally high, and was also high in the main Shi'a areas in the central and southern provinces of the country. In some parts of the country experiencing a degree of insurgency, the turnout was impressive, with many people taking risks in order to vote. Even so, in the main Sunni areas turnout was below ten per cent of the electorate.

A secondary issue was the relatively poor performance of Mr Alawi's party, given that he had been the political leader most favoured by the USA, and this is one aspect of an electoral process that contrasts greatly with original American expectations when the Saddam Hussein regime was terminated nearly two years ago. At that time, there was a confident expectation that a political transition could be overseen in Iraq that would ensure a largely secular government coming to power – what some might call a client regime but Washington would regard as a friendly state that would be committed to a close security relationship with the USA. This would include the very heavy involvement of US companies in the Iraqi oil industry, and an acceptance of the long-term basing of US troops in the country.

Given that Iraqi domestic security is dominantly dependant on the presence of large numbers of US troops, it follows that the US Embassy in Baghdad will have extraordinary influence over whatever administration is established. Even so, this does not disguise the fact that such an administration is not going to be what was expected. Nowhere is this more significant than in relations with Iran. One of the common claims from US sources is that Iran, along with Syria and external paramilitaries, is playing a thoroughly unhelpful role in the evolution of an Iraqi governance that is friendly to the USA. The evidence for the Iranian connection is actually sparse, but what is significant is that the newly elected Iraqi administration is likely to have a particularly sympathetic attitude towards Iran for two reasons.

One is that many of the main political leaders that have won election to the legislature are people who were in exile during the latter stages of the Saddam Hussein regime, with the main place of exile being Iran, not the USA.[1] In providing shelter and some support, Iran is seen intrinsically as helpful to the future development of Shi'a-orientated parties. The second reason is that such Iranian sympathies also apply to Kurdish political elements, if for more pragmatic reasons. For much of the period from 1991 to 2003, the Kurdish region of north-east Iraq operated as a quasi-independent state, aided by the Northern No-Fly Zone that limited the ability of the Saddam Hussein regime to encroach on the area. Although economic and social links with Turkey were important at this time, so were links with Iran, where the Iranian authorities were willing to allow substantial cross-border connections.

The end result of both factors is that there are likely to be personal and political sympathies with Iran felt by the main Shi'a and Kurdish parties in Iraq. This is a long way from US hopes and expectations and is particularly problematic given the manner in which the Iranian nuclear programme has become such a dominant issue in US military planning.

The Insurgency

The election period itself was characterised by singularly forceful action by the US military to close down the risk of electoral disruption by the insurgents. From a US perspective, the results were positive, and there was also a small lull in the insurgency in the few days after the election itself. While it is still only a month since the election, there are two issues that give some idea of the status and effectiveness of the insurgency. One is that, while the number of daily attacks is not quite as high as during the months before the election, they are still sufficient to give a high level of insecurity across much of central Iraq, with extensions to other regions as well.

For US troops, the toll continued to be serious, with fifty-eight killed in February, taking the death toll since the start of the war to almost 1,500. During the course of the month, 450 US soldiers and marines were wounded, 214 of them seriously. For the Iraqi police and security forces, the insurgency continued with little respite, including the bombing of the Tikrit police headquarters, killing at least ten and injuring many more, and a number of assassinations of security officials.[2] On the last day of the month, the worst suicide bomb attack since the start of the war killed 125 people and injured over 100 more outside a police recruitment centre in the city of Hillah, south of Baghdad. One US response to the problems has been a prolonged if little-noticed assault on insurgents in the city of Ramadi.[3]

Another development in many towns in Iraq has been the collapse of neighbourhood councils. The establishment of these, earlier in the occupation, was seen by the Bush administration as a significant step in local governance, but the level of intimidation by insurgents has been such that most no longer operate and many of the members are in hiding.[4]

There has also been a change of tactics by insurgents involving concerted efforts to damage the electricity, oil and water systems.[5] This form of sabotage is not new – there was a particular period during the middle of 2004 when there were persistent pipeline attacks that greatly damaged Iraq's oil export potential, making reconstruction as a whole more difficult. This time, though, the actions of the insurgents are much more specific in that they are systematically concentrated on Baghdad and are having a profound effect on supplies of electricity and petrol to the great majority of the six million people living in the greater Baghdad area. The skill with which the sabotage is conducted shows a thorough knowledge of the entire supply system, suggesting that former officials knowledgeable about the system are involved, or even that inside knowledge of current developments in the system is readily available to insurgents. Given the extent to which the security forces are infiltrated by insurgent elements, this should not cause too much surprise.[6]

While the overall picture emerging is one of substantial post-election problems in curbing the insurgency, the very fact that the elections took place has been seen in the USA as a success for the Bush administration, even if the end result is hardly the one desired. The elections have been followed by two immediate developments in US foreign policy, President Bush's visit to Western Europe and his seeking of a transatlantic consensus over Iran, and a cautious meeting in Slovakia with President Putin of Russia, a political leader who had previously been welcomed by the Bush administration but is now treated with suspicion.

Russia and Iran

During meetings in Belgium and Germany, considerable efforts were made to persuade George W. Bush about the European preference for a diplomatic solution to the potential confrontation with Iran. While there are some in the Bush administration, not least in the State Department, that would greatly prefer to avoid another military confrontation, there is a clear belief in influential neoconservative circles, that Iran must be 'dealt with' early in the second term.[7] In such circumstances, the Europeans may have difficulty in persuading the Iranians to curb their nuclear ambitions, especially as the view among the Washington hawks is that not only must Iran not develop nuclear weapons, it must not develop a nuclear fuel cycle and should not even have a civil nuclear power programme, given the potential for dual use of many nuclear technologies.[8]

What is complicating matters is the involvement of Russia,

with this being the primary reason for the cool state of relations between Washington and Moscow. At the root of this is the agreement signed at the end of the month between Moscow and Tehran, for the provision of uranium fuel for the Bushehr nuclear power plant on the shores of the Persian Gulf. The agreement includes the return of spent fuel rods to Russia, the implication of this being that it will be a closed system in that the Iranians will not be enriching uranium produced from their own mines, and will not have spent fuel available for diverting into plutonium reprocessing. Theoretically, this means that the Bushehr project will not require Iran to operate a nuclear fuel cycle. Even so, opponents in Washington do not accept that such a process can be verified, nor do they accept that Iran even needs to develop a nuclear power programme, given its plentiful reserves of oil and natural gas.

On this last point, the Iranian response is that the country has long had a policy of energy source diversification, including having a substantial component of its electricity supplies produced by hydroelectric power. The claim is made that since Iran does have indigenous sources of uranium-bearing ores, some diversification into nuclear power makes strategic sense. This is questioned in Washington, not least because it implies that obtaining nuclear fuel from Russia is no more than an interim step. Even so, the problem for the USA is that Russia is clearly willing to further develop its relationship with Iran, even if this is against US interests and America's persistent view of Iran as the leading member of the 'axis of evil'.

Awkward Trends

This more generally fits into a pattern in which three major states are developing policies that simply do not fit in with US neoconservative intentions to be the dominant player on the world scene. These states are Russia, China and India, although it is also worth noting a trend in Latin America towards the election of centre-left governments that are cautious about maintaining close relations with the USA, the latest being Uruguay.

The pattern is one of countries taking steps within their capabilities that limit US ambitions. In the case of China and India, there is a particular concern with the long-term security of supplies of oil and natural gas. China still has some domestic sources of fossil fuels, including oil and gas, but has long since passed the point where it could satisfy demand from home supplies. With its very high growth rate, demand for imported oil may now be growing at a rate close to ten per cent a year, and any interruptions of supply could have a substantial and immediate impact on the Chinese economy. As a result, China has been making concerted efforts to identify long-term sources of supply. While some of these efforts are directed at the Caspian Basin, together with overtures being made to some oil-rich African states, the main focus is inevitably the Persian Gulf region, with its concentration of well over sixty per cent of world oil reserves.

Late last year, China agreed a long-term deal with Iran for the supply of oil and natural gas, the latter component being crucial because it makes it feasible for Iran to invest in the relatively expensive liquefied natural gas (LNG) tankers required for shipment. Iran has the second largest reserves of any country (after Russia) but needs to invest in expensive and specialist infrastructure if it is to benefit from these reserves. China appears to have no difficulty in working with the Iranian government.

Nor does India, which has, in parallel with the Chinese, agreed a similar long-term oil and gas supply deal with Tehran.

Two things follow that are problematic for the USA. One is likely to be a reluctance on the part of the Chinese to vote in favour of any obviously anti-Iran resolution sponsored in the UN Security Council by the USA, with the threat of a veto always available if not stated in public. The second issue is that neither India nor China will be likely to acquiesce to any programme of targeted economic sanctions against Iran. In a very real sense, the USA is being constrained by the manner in which the international energy market is evolving.

The Russian involvement in the potential limiting of US influence is rather different, given its plentiful domestic supplies of oil and gas. Here, the issue is one of export potentials, partly for nuclear power but much more obviously for weapons systems. The Russian support for the completion of the Bushehr nuclear power plant in Iran may be causing displeasure in Washington, but this is a rare example of Russia exporting civil nuclear technology. What is much more significant is the nature of Russian arms exports.

At the end of the cold war, the Russian military-industrial complex went into something approaching freefall, as a heavily protected domestic industry suddenly lost almost all its orders because of the near collapse of the Russian economy. Some sectors of the industry hung on by putting much more effort into arms exports, but much of the military equipment was relatively obsolete, there being little money available to undertake the kinds of research and development programmes that could maintain a degree of technological equivalence with the USA.

By the end of the 1990s, the Russian economy had improved

to the extent that domestic arms orders began to flow, but they were certainly not enough to enable manufacturers to modernise production lines and update the end products. To do this and compete with western states, it was necessary to have vibrant overseas arms markets, and the end result has been a determined effort to expand access to such markets. In most cases, the arms exports still do not compare with US or Israeli equipment, but there are notable exceptions.

One example is the SS-N-22 Sunburn supersonic anti-ship cruise missile, the fastest missile of its kind in the world. While essentially developed during the cold war era, it has been upgraded and is available for sale across the world. Because of the speed, the current anti-missile systems on US Navy ships have little time to react, making the ships theoretically vulnerable to SS-N-22 missiles whether launched from land or sea. For Russia, providing such a system for export has three substantial advantages. One is that it brings in much-needed revenues, some of which can be invested in further areas of military technology, and a second is that it enables Russia to improve relations with a range of countries. The third and most valuable asset, though, is that it serves as a potential limitation on US power.

In relation both to energy supplies, especially oil and gas, but also to arms exports, it is apparent that we are moving into a multi-polar world in a manner that has not been fully recognised in the USA and which is beginning to cause some consternation, hence the less than cordial discussions with President Putin. Iran may be one example where a significant state, Russia, simply does not do what the USA requires, but there are likely to be others. This may not mean the end of the drive for a New American Century but it does indicate some of the limitations now being experienced. Neither Russia, India nor even China can begin to match the military power of the USA, nor would they pretend that they could do so. What they are able to do, though, is to develop policies that suit their own economic circumstances, whether these be arms sales or energy agreements, while also having a limiting effect on US power. For all three countries, and from rather different perspectives, these are satisfying outcomes.

Chapter 12
The Bush Administration, Insurgencies and Iran
March 2005

Afghanistan

When the Taliban regime in Afghanistan was terminated towards the end of 2001, two outcomes were expected. One would be a substantial if not terminal weakening of the capabilities of al-Qaeda and its associates. Given that al-Qaeda had training and logistical functions centred largely on Afghanistan, the assumption was that removal of these functions would have a fundamental impact on its potential for further action. Indeed, this was seen in Washington as the appropriate and relevant response to the 9/11 attacks. In the event, the al-Qaeda phenomenon has since undergone a series of transformations. The many associates remain active across the world, the overall level of activity has been higher than before 9/11, and the detention or killing of some leadership elements has had little effect as new cohorts have come forward. In some parts of the world, most notably southern Thailand, there has even been a recent upsurge in activity.

The second expectation was that Afghanistan would be aided to make major and rapid progress in post-war reconstruction, aided by appropriate security support and very substantial development assistance. Whatever else might happen, this would ensure that Afghanistan would not regain its status as the world's primary source of heroin. Over three years later, the situation remains complex, but it cannot be said that progress has been even remotely as strong as had been hoped.

There are three aspects to the current situation across the country. On a positive note, there is an established government under Hamid Karzai, the security situation in Kabul and some other major cities, even if still unstable at times, has improved, and a degree of economic revival, along with the enhancement of a range of development projects, has attracted a large number of exiles back to the country. Even so, Afghanistan remains hugely dependent on international aid, and the Karzai government controls very little of the overall budget. Of the $4.75 billion budget for the new year, over ninety per cent comes from donors and less than ten per cent from internal revenue raising.

Furthermore, the government controls less than a quarter of this budget, the great majority being fed through to nongovernmental organisations and projects run directly by foreign governments. There are currently over 2,000 nongovernmental organisations registered in Afghanistan, with many engaged in development projects. As they frequently employ western specialists at high salaries, there remains considerable ill feeling over the siphoning off of aid into relatively few non-Afghan hands.

The second aspect, which also affects development projects, is that the background insurgency in parts of southern and eastern Afghanistan has continued through a fourth winter, with some

17,000 US combat troops involved in counter-guerrilla warfare and other security functions. Their activities have included large-scale detentions without trial, with these functions apparently conducted without any form of control or oversight by the Karzai administration.[1]

Beyond this is the more substantial national and international issue of Afghanistan's regaining its place as the world's leading source of heroin. This has been directly contrary to the development plans advocated by some coalition governments. In one particular period of Taliban rule, 2000–2001, there were determined and often brutal methods introduced to control opium poppy growing, leading to the almost total collapse of poppy cultivation. The turnaround since then has been remarkable, with the UN Office on Drugs and Crime reporting that Afghanistan now accounts for eighty-seven per cent of worldwide illegal production of heroin.

The Afghan opium export market is now worth $2.8 billion and production is close to the peak years of the early 1990s, including a sixty-four per cent increase last year. The basis of production is particularly robust in that the poppies are grown on around 330,000 plots by small farmers, so much so that about one in ten of the entire Afghan population has some kind of involvement. Given the levels of poverty in Afghanistan, recently listed in 173rd place out of 178 in the Human Development Index, the key issue is that opium poppy cultivation, where soil and climatic conditions are favourable, is hugely more profitable than other crops. Typically, an opium poppy crop will yield twelve times the gross income of wheat.[2]

Although the illicit drug industry in Afghanistan has not reached the levels of control of some South American cartels, drawing profits from all four stages in the process (production, processing, trafficking and retailing), there are indications that existing warlords and new drug entrepreneurs are beginning to adopt similar policies. The US government has recently announced an intensive anti-drug programme for implementation in Afghanistan, but it is highly unlikely that this will prove effective unless in the context of much greater support for rural development. That, for the moment, is simply not forthcoming on the scale required.

Iraq

It is now two years since the second post-9/11 regime termination took place, that of Saddam Hussein in Iraq. In that time over 18,000 civilians have been killed in Iraq, some tens of thousands have been injured and, at any one time, around 10,000 people are detained without trial in Iraq by US and UK forces. Over 1,500 US troops have been killed and a further 11,000 injured, with over 10,000 more evacuated due to physical or mental illness. According to the UN Human Rights Commission, about a quarter of all children in Iraq are not getting enough to eat, and the actual incidence of malnutrition has risen from 4.0 to 7.7 per cent.

Following the elections for the provisional government at the end of January there was a period of chaotic negotiations for the leadership of the government that was largely rationalised by the end of March. During this period there was some evidence of a decrease in the insurgency as far as it was affecting US troops. Thirty-six US soldiers died, the lowest number for a year, although over 350 were injured, around 150 of them seriously.

Around the end of the month, there were some cautiously optimistic statements from US military personnel, suggesting that the insurgency was diminishing and that internal Iraqi security forces would progressively take over many US security roles, with the US forces increasingly being used to provide emergency cover. Against this, other analysts frankly doubted that there was any short-term possibility of the poorly equipped and rapidly trained Iraqi forces taking a major role. Moreover, the insurgency itself continued to take a heavy toll of Iraqi political and security personnel, not least through numerous assassinations of senior security officers and civil servants. There were also indications that the insurgents were developing new tactics, including an ability to mount large-scale attacks against heavily protected US facilities, a substantial raid against the Abu Ghraib prison at the end of the month that injured forty-four US troops being an example.

The Bush Second Term

Although reporting from Iraq in the US media is now restricted to occasional major events, the slow but steady reporting of deaths and injuries among US soldiers through local newspapers and TV and radio stations across the USA is having a cumulative effect, leading to a decline in support for the war. This has been countered by a heavy emphasis from the administration on the January elections, and the subsequent, if slow, establishment of a provisional Iraqi government. The problems in Iraq and Afghanistan have certainly not had any discernible impact on the determination of the Bush administration to consolidate the neoconservative position in the wider international sphere.

Although not a neoconservative in the strict sense, the decision to appoint John Bolton as US Ambassador to the United Nations is one indication, given his strong views on the need for the US to

117

pursue its own interests often regardless of treaty commitments.[3] Another is the appointment of the former US Ambassador to Iraq, John Negroponte, as overall head of security and intelligence.

Perhaps most notable is the appointment of the former Deputy Secretary for Defence, Paul Wolfowitz, as the new head of the World Bank. This is perhaps the clearest indication of the intention of the administration to promote its economic ideology in the wider international community. Although the World Bank is far from being the lead player in global development, there is a strong symbolism in this appointment, establishing a neoconservative vision for an organisation that has considerable influence across the field of international development.

Iran and the Non-Proliferation Treaty

The extension of vigorous unilateralist and neoconservative policies more formally into the international arena is clearly central to the second George W. Bush administration and it is probable that an early effect of this will be the issue of Iran in relation to the Non-Proliferation Treaty (NPT), especially as the treaty's next five-yearly review conference will take place in a few weeks time.

The NPT was opened for signing back in 1968 and entered into force in 1970. Thirty-five years later, there are 189 signatories, making it one of the most widely accepted multilateral treaties. Three key states have never been members, Israel, India and Pakistan, and one state, North Korea, has withdrawn. A second limitation to the treaty is that Article Six requires members that already have nuclear weapons – the USA, Russia, China, France and the UK – to progressively give up their nuclear weapons. Although there were substantial cutbacks on nuclear weapons after the end of the cold war, all five states are involved in nuclear modernisation and none has seriously embraced its commitments under the treaty. Even so, there is a very widespread international consensus that the NPT has helped control nuclear proliferation, limiting it to just nine states when many analysts back in the 1980s would have expected many more candidate states by now.

The problem is that there is a bargain at the heart of the treaty that is now becoming unacceptable to the USA and risks severe damage to the treaty itself. At the time the treaty was originally negotiated in the late 1960s, civil nuclear power was still expanding rapidly. It was recognised, though, that the technologies relevant to civil nuclear power programmes were closely linked to those suitable for nuclear weapons programmes. Indeed it later became clear that the world's first civil nuclear power plant, Calder Hall in the UK, was primarily a system for producing plutonium for Britain's nuclear weapons programme.

At the time, nuclear power programmes were thought to be safe and economical methods of generating electricity that appealed to countries seeking to promote the rapid development of their electric power systems. As a result, a core element of the treaty was a willingness to allow member states to do this, provided there was a degree of inspection from the International Atomic Energy Agency (IAEA) to ensure that there were no technological diversions into nuclear weapons programmes.

This 'bargain' has largely held for the past thirty years or so, but is no longer acceptable to the USA, because of its concern over Iran. The Iranians are developing a small nuclear power programme, including the 1,000 MW Bushehr power plant being built by Russia. This plant will use enriched uranium supplied by Russia, but Iran has its own uranium ore deposits and is developing a capability for uranium enrichment that could be used in a future expansion of its nuclear power programme.

It would be technically possible for Iran to develop this programme to produce highly enriched weapons-grade uranium, and other facilities may be under development that could reprocess reactor waste to produce plutonium. It would therefore be possible for Iran to deploy both the uranium and plutonium routes to nuclear weapons if it so decided. This is unacceptable to the Bush administration to the extent that Washington is not prepared to allow the Iranians to have a civil uranium enrichment programme, even though this is allowed under the terms of the NPT.

In part, this is because of the administration's 'axis of evil' approach and its belief in the need to pre-empt future threats, but it is supported by evidence that Iran has been tardy in its dealings with the IAEA, with an evident reluctance to be fully forthcoming on the extent of its civil nuclear programmes. Critics of the US position point to two other states that have also been less than open with the IAEA – South Korea and Egypt – but both of these states are closely allied to the USA and face none of the pressures now being put on Tehran.

The view of the Bush administration now appears to be that the Non-Proliferation Treaty is so flawed that it is in conflict with US security interests. It is an issue that may well come to a head during the review conference in New York in May, especially if the US delegation asserts the right to take independent action against Iran at some time in the near future. The timescale is relatively short – if a major crisis were to develop between the USA, or indeed Israel, and Iran, then the worst-case scenario of military action against Iranian nuclear facilities would entail action before the middle of 2006. By that time, the Bushehr nuclear power station will be fully fuelled and will be close to operational. An attack on such a facility could have Chernobyl-level consequences with a risk of regional contamination stretching across western Gulf States such as Saudi Arabia, Kuwait and the United Arab Emirates.[4]

It is therefore the case that the forthcoming NPT review conference will be a substantial test for the treaty itself and for the attitude of the Bush administration to multilateral efforts to control nuclear weapons proliferation. Given the fact that John Bolton is well known for his opposition to most forms of multilateral arms control, it would be wise to expect the USA to seek major modifications or else to give a clear indication of its intentions to take future counter-proliferation actions in its own interests, whatever the dangerous consequences for multilateral approaches.

Chapter 13
The Iraq Impasse
April 2005

Comical Ali

The termination of the Saddam Hussein regime came after a brief but bitter three-week conflict in March and April 2003, that phase of the war ending with the American occupation of Baghdad and the disappearance of most of the members of the old regime. One of the most remarkable features of the final days of the regime was the behaviour of the Information Minister, Mohammed Saeed al-Sahaf, ever ready to report to the journalists in Baghdad that the regime was resisting the occupation to great effect.

Even when US forces were in the heart of Baghdad, he insisted that their progress was slow and that they were suffering great casualties. He was dubbed 'Comical Ali'. Mr al-Sahaf disappeared shortly after the US occupation of Baghdad but surfaced three months later to give an interview for the Dubai-based Al-Arabiya TV station, claiming to have been detained in Baghdad and then released by US forces, a claim denied by the US authorities.

At the height of the fighting in Baghdad, one of Mr al-Sahaf's final claims was to the effect that 'we will bury you' – a US occupation of Iraq would lead to a bitter conflict that would be immensely costly to US forces. Like almost all of his other statements, this was dismissed out of hand and, only three weeks later, President Bush declared military operations over.

During those first three weeks of the war, Mr al-Sahaf became a figure of fun, although there were already anomalies that suggested that regime termination would not mark the end of the conflict. Although there was intense fighting between US forces and Republican Guard units south of Baghdad and around the city's international airport, one of the remarkable features of the conflict was the almost total absence of Saddam Hussein's elite forces, including the Special Republican Guard, some commando units and the various military forces under the control of the security and intelligence agencies. There had been an assumption before the start of the war that these would be the key forces defending Baghdad and the heart of the regime. In the event they were nowhere to be seen as the regime collapsed, having apparently melted away with weapons largely intact. While most of Mr al-Sahaf's comments were wild exaggerations, it is possible that he was aware of this development and knew that a guerrilla war was planned. Certainly it is one element of all his comments that now strikes a chord two years later, with the war continuing with renewed intensity.

Because the initial termination of the Saddam Hussein regime was so rapid, there was an immediate tendency to describe the conflict in Iraq as a three-week war followed by a period of instability and insurgency. In this interpretation, the earlier 1991 war was a six-week conflict to evict the Iraqis from Kuwait and the 2003 war took half that time to terminate the regime or to 'finish the job'. This representation of events was made more viable by the fact that it took several weeks after the fall of the regime for the insurgency to develop – in the months of May and June 2003, the US forces lost only sixty-seven troops, one of the lowest figures for any such period since the onset of the conflict. At the same time, such an interpretation is deeply misleading, in that a short war followed by a difficult peace implies that the problems in Iraq are essentially short-term. A much stronger argument can be made for the idea that the initial three-week period marked the start of a prolonged conflict that is now in its third year. In such a context, some of Mr al-Sahaf's comments are strangely prescient.

Even so, in the two years since the termination of the Saddam Hussein regime there have been many occasions when the US military and political authorities have declared the insurgency to be in retreat. These have included the period around the killing of Qusay and Uday Hussein in July 2003, the capture of Saddam Hussein himself in December of that year, the establishment of Mr Alawi's interim administration the following June and the focus on Fallujah as the centre of insurgency last November. In every case, the optimism was short-lived, yet it surfaced again at the time of the elections in January.

Insurgency Renewed

In the analysis for January (Chapter 10), the three-month period after the elections, from February to April, was thought to be a key period for understanding whether the insurgency would continue to develop or whether the political process would undermine support for the insurgents. At the end of that three months, the conclusion has to be broadly pessimistic, indeed the last week of April was marked by a period of sustained violence, and the previous month saw some 250 members of the Iraqi police and security forces, including many new recruits, killed by insurgents.

There was certainly a brief lull in the insurgency in the immediate aftermath of the January elections, although hindsight suggests that this was largely due to the limitations on insurgent movements through an intense period of US military control around the time of the elections, a degree of control that simply could not be maintained for any length of time, given the size of the occupation forces.[1] Furthermore, it has become clear that the insurgents themselves have changed their tactics to concentrate primarily on the Iraqi security forces.

Attacks on US forces certainly continue, and now include occasional major assaults on US bases, sometimes involving more than fifty insurgents in single operations.[2] The US casualties remain high – during the course of March and April, US forces lost eighty-eight people and, in the eight-week period to 26 April, nearly 950 US troops were wounded, 255 of them seriously.[3] At the same time, it is the Iraqi security and police forces that are bearing the brunt of the insurgency, and in substantial parts of Iraq such forces have withdrawn to the relative safety of bases that are often outside the towns and cities that they are meant to control.

There are several factors that help to explain the continuing development of the insurgency and these need to be explored to get some indication of probable trends in the coming months. One key issue is the enduring and intense hostility towards US forces of a substantial minority of the Iraqi population, combined with a broad antagonism to occupation by the majority. Even now, two years after an apparent liberation, there is a clear majority view that the US forces are occupiers rather than liberators and should leave as soon as possible. One problem is that the incoming interim government is hopelessly weak in terms of providing internal security and is entirely dependent on the presence of foreign troops for its survival. Since this dependence is primarily on US military units, the new government has a potential credibility problem in that it can be readily seen as a client regime of Washington.

In practice, this is what it is – in addition to the US military presence, it is the funding from Washington that is paying for much of the functioning of the government, and US advisers permeate all the major sectors of government. Furthermore, some of the incoming politicians, notably the new Deputy Prime Minister, Ahmad Chalabi, have been closely connected with the USA for many years, even if many politicians have rather closer links with Tehran than Washington.

The political situation is also complicated by the failure between Shi'a and Sunni political figures to agree to senior ministries for Sunni politicians, emphasising the view that the government is being 'sown up' by Shi'a leaders subject to US influence. This may not be fully accurate but it is a damaging perception, adding to a sense of alienation among Sunni communities that formed the national elite under the old regime.

A second factor is the behaviour and tactics of the US troops. Since the start of the war, the US has had nearly 1,600 troops killed and over 12,000 wounded, with at least that number evacuated because of non-combat injuries and physical and mental ill-health. While nothing like the casualties of Vietnam or

Korea, the effect on a much smaller army has been considerable. Moreover, a largely urban-based insurgency results in formidable unpredictability for the US troops and a persistent trend of response with heavy firepower. As a result of this, civilian casualties continue to mount, with cautious estimates such as those of the Iraq Body Count group suggesting that civilian deaths are heading towards 25,000, with a substantial number caused by US military action.[4]

The tendency to shoot first is inevitable, given the vulnerability of US troops and the availability of overwhelming firepower, but its effect is to further strengthen support for insurgents, especially in those substantial regions of Iraq where the insurgency is most intense. The assault on Fallujah last November was a notable case, and that city is now beginning to acquire an iconic status across the Arab world that is reminiscent of the impact of *Guernica* across Europe in the late 1930s.

Fallujah itself remains a largely wrecked city, even five months after the assault. By mid-April only 90,000 of the 250,000 inhabitants had returned to the city, with many of the others still camped out in refugee settlements. A quarter of the houses in the whole city, some 10,000, were destroyed in the bombardment and another 10,000 were damaged. The majority of the city still did not have electricity supplies or piped water, unemployment was estimated at eighty-five per cent, and the economy was largely moribund. For the residents who have returned, the city remains under extraordinarily strict control by US forces. There are only four checkpoint routes in and out of the city, residents have to queue for up to four hours and there is a 7 p.m. daily curfew.

Although Iraqi security forces may be involved in controlling the city, it is the US forces that are clearly in charge of the whole operation and the inference is that this is a city under the near-total control of foreign occupiers. The view is thus of the 'city of mosques' subjected to a formidable military assault last November which killed hundreds of people and has left it largely in ruins while remaining under American occupation.

From a US standpoint, the Fallujah assault was an absolute necessity, given the intensity of the insurgency and the belief that Fallujah was at its centre. The effect, though, has been to further reinforce the view across much of Iraq that this was yet another example of fundamental external control by forces determined to use as much military firepower as might prove necessary to control what is widely seen as legitimate resistance to occupation.

These three factors – the political uncertainty following the elections, a perception of Iraq as a client state, and the use of force by US troops – all help to explain the continuing intensity of the insurgency, but do not fully indicate the nature of the insurgents themselves. One major feature is the near-daily use of suicide bombers, suggesting that there are hundreds of people, mostly young men, who are sufficiently dedicated to be willing to give up their lives. What is not clear is the extent to which the suicide bombers come from within the Iraqi population or are made up primarily of foreign paramilitaries for whom Iraq has quickly become the centre of the war against foreign forces in the Arab world, replacing Afghanistan quicker than anyone might have expected.

From the limited evidence available, only a small minority of the insurgents are from other countries, perhaps as few as ten per cent, although there is some evidence that paramilitary recruits from the western Gulf states and North Africa enter

Iraq for periods of weeks or months to gain training and combat experience, before returning to their own countries to work in opposition to local elites.

Within Iraq itself, part of the insurgency is being mounted by foreign paramilitaries, a small faction continues the radical Islamic paramilitary activities that were present during the Saddam Hussein regime, and there appear to be large numbers of supporters coming from elements best described as Sunni nationalists. Beyond this, though, much of the core of the insurgency stems from Ba'athist elements, many of which went to ground in the final days of the old regime. Most of them have substantial military training, including insurgency tactics, they have massive quantities of weapons and munitions available and they believe that they can force the US military to leave Iraq and even establish a neo-Ba'athist regime.

In the long run, it is a forlorn outlook – Iraq has far too much oil for US forces to leave in their entirety, the Kurdish north-east of the country would resist such a regime with a profound intensity and Iran would be bitterly opposed to such an emergence. At the same time, it is an outlook that will be extremely difficult to counter, even given the demographic realities of the Ba'athists coming from a small minority of the population.[5]

Given the current intensity of the insurgency, it is possible that the next few months will see an agreement on the formation of an interim government that will include significant Sunni political figures in key ministerial positions. It is just possible that this will begin the process of undermining support for the insurgents. On the other hand, this is only meant to be an interim administration and it has already served three of its intended eleven months without being able to function as planned. Furthermore, the insurgents have access to almost unlimited quantities of supplies and their current level of activity is about as high as at any time in the past two years.

Beyond this there is one enduring and uncomfortable issue – Iraq is seen across the region as a major Arab state, at the heart of the Arab world, that is under a forceful and, in all probability, long-term foreign occupation. At the very least that must be seen as an unpredictable factor, but certainly one that suggests that a political solution to the insurgency is going to be extremely difficult to find.

Chapter 14
Iraq and the War on Terror
Year Two

Initial Optimism

In May 2004, it was still possible to argue that the insurgency in Iraq might be brought under control by conventional methods of counter-insurgency warfare. The previous twelve months had not been easy for the USA and its coalition partners, and each of the periods of optimism during the course of the year had been proved to be false. Indeed, April 2004 had been one of the most difficult months since the termination of the Saddam Hussein regime, with major conflict in Fallujah following the killing of four US security contractors.

Although the United States military used considerable force in countering the insurgents in the city, they eventually withdrew following an uneasy ceasefire and their replacement by Iraqi units. Within weeks, though, Fallujah was once more under insurgent control, and this was indicative of a developing pattern in the insurgency. US forces were frequently able to take control of towns, cities or rural districts, but did not have sufficient personnel to maintain control, nor were Iraqi units capable of taking over security, for reasons of morale, equipment, training, leadership or all of these.

Nevertheless, by May 2004, there was still some sense of optimism in US political circles. In terms of domestic politics, the problems in Iraq were not having a particularly damaging effect on President Bush as he approached the task of seeking re-election. In part this was due to the reluctance of his opponent, Senator John Kerry, to raise this issue as a core part of his campaign, not least because of the risk of being labelled unpatriotic. It was also a result of the surprisingly little publicity being given in most organs of the media to the deaths and injuries being suffered by US forces in Iraq. From the start of the war, the Bush administration had sought to minimise publicity for flights bringing back the bodies of fallen soldiers, or to publicise the casualty evacuation flights coming back to the United States of America every week.

In Iraq itself, US military and political leaders also expressed a degree of optimism. Many people in the military within the country still believed the insurgency could be brought under control through military operations. There was also a belief in political circles that the transition to an Iraqi administration might undercut support for the insurgency, however limited might be such an administration's capacity for independent action because of the overwhelming US role in security and its substantial involvement in the civil infrastructure and political process. In other words, while it was recognised that the insurgency had become much more persistent and deep-seated than had been anticipated, there was an expectation that the second year after regime termination would bring a much greater degree of stability.

This has not proved to be the case. Instead, the insurgency has persisted throughout the second year of the war, has evolved in a number of significant ways and appears as robust as ever. The civil reconstruction of Iraq after more than a decade of sanctions and a violent overthrow of the Saddam Hussein regime has proved to be deeply problematic and has been made much more difficult by the persistent targeting of the economic infrastructure by insurgents. Attacks directed against the oil facilities and electricity supplies have been particularly damaging and have even resulted in periods of severe fuel shortages in a country that is second only to Saudi Arabia in the size of its oil reserves.

Casualties among US military personnel increased in the twelve months to the end of April 2005, with 847 killed compared with 601 for the previous twelve months.[1] This was despite a marked tendency for the US forces to limit the numbers of their patrols, to substantially increase the levels of protection available to their troops and to consolidate their presence in a smaller number of well-protected sites, compared with the widespread nature of the basing system in operation shortly after the termination of the Saddam Hussein regime. Casualties among Iraqi citizens now number around 25,000 killed and tens of thousands seriously injured.[2] While many of the more recent casualties have resulted from insurgent activity, a high proportion of the deaths since March 2003 have been caused by coalition actions.

This chapter will seek to analyse the main reasons for the persistence of the insurgency within the complexity of a multiethnic Iraqi society and, in doing so, will suggest the range of choices open to the Bush administration as it heads towards the second year of its second term. It will then go on to place the developments in Iraq in the wider context of the war on terror.

Insurgency and Response

Over the last year, as before, there have been repeated assertions from US sources that much of the driving force for the insurgency has come from outside Iraq, with the confrontation therefore being part of the wider US global war on terror. Abu Musab al-Zarqawi has frequently been cited as a key figure in the insurgency, and his supposedly close links with Osama bin Laden have been given as evidence of the Iraq/war on terror connection. It has also been suggested that Islamic paramilitaries, especially those crossing into Iraq from Syria, have been core constituents of the insurgency.

Al-Zarqawi and other foreign paramilitaries have certainly played a significant role in the developing insurgency, but the hard evidence of their being substantive elements is difficult to come by. In terms of those detained, foreign paramilitaries make up a very small part of the insurgency, estimated by the US Army to be about 500 to 2,000 in number.[3] Where there is a greater significance is in the proportion of suicide or martyr bombers who are coming from abroad, and this may be substantially higher than the proportion among the insurgents as a whole. In relation to the overall situation:

The government faces an insurgency estimated at between 20,000 and 50,000 strong. These fighters are organised in as many as 70 cells, operating largely independently and at best with attenuated coordination. With no coherent centre of gravity and no overall leadership, the insurgency cannot be defeated simply by the application of brute force.[4]

Another assessment gives a broadly similar picture but in a wider context of the nature of the more general support:

> They have a lot of money, stashed before the fall of Saddam Hussein; they have legions of former Republican Guard and *Mukhabarat* (intelligence) officers (the guerrillas have at least 40,000 active members, plus a supporting cast of 80,000); they have loads of weapons (at least 250,000 tons remaining); they can enjoy a non-stop flow of financing, especially from Saudi Arabia and the Gulf; and they can count on crucial tactical support by a few hundred Arab jihadis.[5]

This estimate of the availability of munitions may be high, but there appears to have been little of no limitation on insurgent activity stemming from any shortage. Indeed, there have been occasions in the past year when it was cheaper for arms dealers elsewhere in the region to buy weapons from sources in Iraq then in neighbouring countries. At some stage, there may be a requirement for insurgents to import weapons from surrounding countries, but that stage has not been reached in any systematic manner. What has certainly become clear, well over two years since the termination of the Saddam Hussein regime, is that the stockpiles of munitions and weapons available in Iraq, and their ready availability to opponents of occupation, have become a much more significant factor in the persistence of the insurgency than had ever been expected. Given US capabilities in satellite and aerial reconnaissance, including the use of drones, it is probable that the arms supplies are dispersed into many small dumps. That this is possible does once again suggest a degree of community support that had not been anticipated.

As to the overall make-up of the insurgents, the main elements appear to be drawn from Ba'athist elements, especially from elite sectors of the old regime's armed forces and security organisations, in lose alliance with Sunni Islamic radicals. In addition, there may be growing numbers of insurgents and supporters, drawn principally but not solely, from the Sunni community, who are acting from more nationalist motives, both Sunni and Iraqi nationalism.

Motivations

The motivations for the insurgency are numerous, and it is not easy to rank them, not least because they are evolving. The extreme disorder, especially the widespread looting, experienced immediately after the termination of the Saddam Hussein regime, had an early effect in that it demonstrated that the liberators, as they saw themselves, could not maintain control. While this was fairly short-lived, it was followed by a marked rise in crime, especially in the major centres of population, which has proved very difficult to control. Robberies, kidnappings and other crimes against property and persons have persisted at a very high level and have again demonstrated the incapacity of the occupying forces and their Iraqi government associates to maintain order.

This has been compounded by the exceptionally slow rate of reconstruction, made worse by constant insecurity and sabotage. Even the manner in which foreign contractors and labour have been brought in has been a source of dissatisfaction, especially when there have been Iraqi contractors and very large numbers of unemployed Iraqis readily available.

For the most part, those sections of the Iraqi community that have been most supportive of the insurgency have been Sunnis, but the impact of the slow pace of reconstruction has had its effect across the whole of Iraq apart from Iraqi Kurdish areas in the north-east of the country that have long had a high degree of political and economic independence. For the Shi'a majority, there have been substantial occasions of resistance, not least in Najaf and the Sadr City district of Baghdad, but most of the insurgency activity stems from the Sunni community from which Saddam Hussein formerly drew so much of his power. That community, being a fairly small minority in Iraq as a whole, has a strong feeling of vulnerability, made worse by the contrast between this and its previous elite position.

What is striking, as discussed earlier, is the emergence of a pattern of insurgency that, as with the dispersal of arms dumps, suggests substantial community support rather than a degree of isolation. It is demonstrated by the manner in which, on numerous occasions, insurgents have been able to respond to major counter-insurgency operations by US and Iraqi government forces in particular areas. Time and again, a degree of resistance has been offered, and the majority of insurgents have been dispersed; immediately, however, they or other insurgents have gone on the offensive elsewhere. It has also been noticeable how US and Iraqi government forces may have been able to take control of towns or cities but have been unable to maintain control once the majority of the forces have been deployed elsewhere to counter other insurgent actions.

Aiding the Insurgency

Two other factors are aiding the insurgency – the nature of US military operations and the manner in which Iraq is seen elsewhere in the Islamic world as a confrontation worthy of support. The USA has professional volunteer armed forces in Iraq, not conscripts, but these young people are not fighting the kind of conventional war for which they have been trained. Instead, they are facing largely unseen opponents frequently able to attack them with roadside bombs, light mortars, rocket-propelled grenades, sniper fire and suicide bombs. There is systematic and constant uncertainty that even extends to heavily guarded garrisons and, on occasions, the Green Zone itself.[6]

The US casualties, numbering 1,700 killed and over 10,000 seriously injured, may be far lower than in Vietnam, but the Vietnam War was fought with a massively larger conscript army. In Iraq, the numbers are far smaller, and the injuries often involve people being maimed for life. At the same time, the US forces are heavily armed and can readily call up artillery, helicopter gunships and strike aircraft. Because of the opponents they face, there is very strong pressure to use the firepower advantage, but this inevitably leads to large numbers of civilian deaths and injuries.

Moreover, such firepower is not spread across Iraq as a whole but is now concentrated very much in the Sunni-populated regions, except when there have been major confrontations with Shi'a militia, as in Najaf in August 2004. Earlier in the war, especially in the first three weeks leading to regime termination, most of the conflict was in the south of the country, as were the casualties. In more recent months, a higher proportion of casualties have been within the Sunni minority, a community of fewer than seven million people. As a consequence, a large part of that minority will have personal experience of such casualties, either through extended families, neighbourhoods or friendships.

The second issue, that of wider regional support, is important because it provides a stream of dedicated paramilitary activists, many of them prepared to be suicide bombers, as well as substantial financial assistance. What is not easy to unravel is the extent to which support for Iraqi opposition to what is seen across the region as US occupation, dovetails with support for the al-Qaeda movement and its affiliates. One aspect of the current war is the manner in which it is covered by the evolving Arab media, especially satellite news channels such as Al Jazeera and numerous web sites.

The 1991 Gulf War was characterised, in media terms, as the 'CNN War', with coverage of that war dominated by western interests; it has been suggested that the current war is better seen as the 'Al Jazeera War'.[7] The USA has certainly tried to dominate the news media, not least through the extensive practice of embedding reporters with military units and, at the same time, restricting access to 'independents'. Such tactics have undoubtedly been of real value in presenting the administration's interpretation of the war to domestic audiences within the USA, and has also had some effect across the western media as a whole.

By contrast, the news coverage by satellite channels across the Middle East has been radically different, both in the coverage of Afghanistan and Iraq and also in terms of news coverage of the ongoing Israeli/Palestinian confrontation. The effect has been both considerable and unexpected, at least for the Bush administration, in that it has presented a picture of opposition to occupation that contrasts markedly with the US domestic media.

There are occasions, though, when representations from both 'sides' serve to give a comprehensive picture, and one such example was the assault on Fallujah in November 2004. Although very little television footage of the effects of the assault became available even to the Arab news channels, their previous coverage of US actions against other urban areas had given copious examples of the impact of US military firepower. Because Fallujah was regarded by the US military as a core focus of the insurgency, there was a willingness to have TV crews readily available as the assault progressed, the end result being several nights of TV coverage showing massive quantities of munitions being poured into the city.

It later became apparent that more than half of the houses in the city of nearly 300,000 people had been damaged, with perhaps half of those destroyed. Together with damage to most of the mosques, schools and public buildings, it was evident that, even without detailed TV images, the 'city of mosques' had experienced an extraordinary assault. Moreover, as the following months showed, this assault had little effect on the further development of the insurgency, with substantial insurgent activity breaking out in Mosul even as the Fallujah operation was still under way.

The overall effect of US military tactics, whether used against Fallujah, Najaf, Ramadi, Qaim or other towns and cities, has been to greatly increase regional antagonism to the USA, at the very least increasing wider support for the insurgents, and possibly having a more general effect on recruitment into radical Islamic movements that may be evolving and operating far beyond Iraq. Perhaps what is most surprising is the apparent lack of recognition in the Bush administration, of the manner in which the Iraq war is an aid to the evolution of radical Islamic movements across the world even though experienced analysts in the USA have made just this point.[8]

If we add the two factors just discussed – the counterproductive effect of US use of heavy military firepower, with widening support for the insurgency across the region – to the internal dynamics of the insurgency, it is reasonable to conclude that the USA is in very serious difficulties in Iraq, and senior members of the military, and of the administration, are now coming to accept that the US military, with all its capabilities, is not able to defeat the insurgents. In April 2005, for example, General Richard Myers, Chair of the US Joint Chiefs of Staff, acknowledged that the insurgency had not diminished in the previous twelve months,[9] and, in an interview on BBC TV's *Newsnight* on 14 June, the Secretary of Defense, Donald Rumsfeld, commented:

> This insurgency is going to be defeated not by the coalition
> – it's going to be defeated by the Iraqi security forces, and
> that is going to happen as the Iraq people begin to believe
> that they've got a future in that country.[10]

In a further comment, a few days later, Mr Rumsfeld expressed the view that insurgencies such as that in Iraq could take up to ten or twelve years to overcome, an apparent admission that the world's most powerful army was finding it very difficult, if not impossible, to resolve the Iraq conflict.

A Coalition of the Willing?

One of the features of US policy since the war started in March 2003 has been to emphasise that the operation has been a multinational coalition of willing states, with more than twenty providing military resources in Iraq. This coalition has been much smaller than the coalition in 1991, and most member states have committed hundreds rather than thousands of troops. Even so, it has been an important aspect of the military posture insofar as it has suggested a degree of international legitimacy. Four countries have continued to be important in this context – Britain, Italy, Poland and Ukraine, but one of the features of the second year of the war has been the decline in support for the war in these countries with clear signs by the middle of 2005 that the coalition was in marked decline. By July 2005, Italy, Poland and Ukraine had all indicated their intention of withdrawing their forces in Iraq, and there was even an indication that Britain planned to scale down its forces by perhaps seventy-five per cent. In the case of Britain, this may be linked to an intention to commit substantially larger forces to Afghanistan than are currently present, and this, combined with problems of 'overstretch' within the British Army, may provide an explanation for this change of policy on the part of President Bush's closest ally.

It is also the case that Britain's support for the war in Iraq had a substantial impact on the General Election campaign in May 2005. Although the Labour Party was returned to power, its majority was much reduced, although its electoral success was greatly aided by the presence of two major opposition parties splitting the anti-government vote. Mr Blair, in particular, lost substantial support, largely over questions of trust that were directly related to the war. While support for Mr Bush is likely to be maintained by Mr Blair in the new parliament, the experience of that election campaign indicates that the US conduct of the war in Iraq is unlikely to command majority public support in Britain.

US Options in Iraq

In such circumstances, what are the options open to the USA in Iraq? There are five reasonably distinct possibilities – defeat of the insurgency, redeployment of US forces in Iraq away from the cities, a US defeat and precipitate withdrawal, a planned withdrawal with substantial UN support or a long-term conflict with an uncertain outcome.

Looking at the first possibility, if the insurgency could be brought under control within a year or so, this might be through some combination of the rapid onset of political stability based on inclusion of the Sunni community, coupled with the successful deployment of Iraqi security forces and hugely improved counter-insurgency capabilities by US forces. For the USA, its military presence would be rapidly consolidated into perhaps 20,000 troops at four main bases, together with a substantial force involved in further training of Iraqi security forces. The wider political result would be the governing of Iraq by an administration that would essentially be a client regime of Washington, given the very powerful influence of the US Embassy in Baghdad, the penetration of US advisers into so many parts of the Iraqi government and the guarantee of future security for that government provided by a continuing US military presence, both in Iraq and neighbouring Kuwait.

Such an outcome would necessarily involve a long-term US military presence in the region, and would be a welcome conclusion for the Bush administration to a difficult operation that would ensure pervasive US influence in the Persian Gulf, even to the extent of discouraging Iran from any policies deemed inappropriate by Washington. Such an outcome presupposes the rapid control of the insurgency in Iraq, and all the current indicators point against this. Even in the best-case scenario, from a US standpoint, the long-term presence of US forces would act as a magnet for Islamic paramilitaries, whether linked directly to the al-Qaeda movement or not. Such groups are not operating on a week-to-week or month-to-month basis, but see their confrontations with foreign occupation forces and local elite regimes as measured in decades. A US military presence operating over a similar timescale would stimulate radical paramilitary responses for as long as it was there.

The second possibility would involve the maintenance of a substantial US military presence in Iraq, but with that presence concentrated away from the cities and especially in those parts of Iraq in which the main oil reserves are located. Such a force would largely disengage from major counter-insurgency operations, leaving those to the Iraqi security forces, although it would have sufficient capability to provide a back-up to such forces. By concentrating on securing Iraq's petroleum wealth, the diminished US military presence of perhaps less than half the current forces, would essentially mean accepting that many towns and cities in central Iraq would fall under the control of insurgents, leading to the possibility of a civil war. At the same time, US casualties would be much lower, and the emphasis would be on the security of the oilfields, with high levels of protection for the production and transport facilities. By controlling the core features of Iraqi national wealth, and thereby its development potential, the USA might eventually be in a position to facilitate negotiations between an Iraqi government and insurgent groups, leading ultimately to some kind of political compromise.

The development of four permanent bases does already point to this as a policy option,[11] but it would be an uncomfortable position, even if more realistic than trying to control the insurgency. Where it would most likely prove unworkable is that substantial military forces would be required to secure the oil-supply routes, the insurgency might evolve in a form that could not be limited by the use of airpower and other support for the Baghdad government, and there might even be a violent change of regime, bringing to power neo-Ba'athists or another deeply anti-American regime. In such circumstances, a further effort at regime termination might be required, with all the military and civilian consequences that this would entail. Even if there was not such a regime change, there is no guarantee of a diminishing insurgency, and the sizeable US presence in Iraq would still act as a magnet for the broader regional groupings of Islamic paramilitaries. From their perspective, it would still be seen as a neo-Christian occupation, in alliance with Zionist Israel, that was seeking long-term control of Arab oil.

The third possibility is a precipitate withdrawal from Iraq following a fundamental shift in policy in Washington that recognises the disastrous nature of the Iraq policy. Whatever the outcome of such a policy shift in Iraq, be that a civil war or even the rapid emergence of a neo-Ba'athist regime, such a withdrawal would at least bring to an end the continuing loss of life and injuries among US forces and the growing domestic antagonism to the Iraq war.

Such a change of policy is unlikely but not impossible. One of the developments during the early months of 2005 was the beginning of a change in the public mood in the USA, with a marked decline in support for the war in Iraq. Even with George W. Bush's re-election only a few months earlier, there was a substantial shift taking place in public opinion in two respects.

One is that there is growing opposition to the war itself and the other is that a large proportion of Americans does not feel that the Iraq policy is making the USA any safer.

Although the ongoing violence in Iraq hardly features on the network news channels unless there is a particularly major incident, the effect of the sheer numbers of casualties is becoming much more prominent across the country in a quite different way. With 1,700 troops killed and many thousands evacuated back to the USA with long-term and often severe disabilities, this is bringing home to people the costs of the war on a township or city district basis. More than 10,000 families and far larger numbers of friends and more distant relatives have been directly affected by the war in this manner, and while their predicaments and frequent unhappiness are not addressed in the national media, they are picked up by local newspapers and radio and TV stations. The end result is a growing awareness, at community level, of the human costs of the war to the US armed forces. This is coming at a time when some of the leading independent analysts and some senior military are questioning the US military posture in Iraq, even to the extent of querying its long-term viability.

It would be quite wrong to claim that this amounts to sufficient political pressure to result in a real change in policy, but it is certainly the case that a further increase in the intensity of the insurgency could make this a central issue during the second George W. Bush administration. Furthermore, there have been clear indications of a decrease in influence among neoconservative elements in the State Department, with this likely to affect State Department orientations on both Iraq and Iran.[12] Against this, though, are the consequences of a precipitate withdrawal from Iraq. Were this to happen, and given the central importance of the security of Persian Gulf oil reserves, the USA would be facing its biggest foreign-policy reversal in decades. Some analysts point to the withdrawal from Vietnam at the end of a much longer and far more costly war, leaving behind a weak government that could not long survive. Withdrawal from Iraq might well have the same effect, and this would be far more significant than the Vietnam withdrawal in that it would cripple the entire US policy for ensuring Gulf security, with implications for the whole idea of a New American Century. In such a context, the idea of a rapid withdrawal is highly unlikely unless there were to be a calamitous increase in US casualties in Iraq.

The possibility of a planned withdrawal, perhaps over two years, involving the insertion of a substantial UN peace-enforcing presence, has been muted and might, in current circumstances, be the option that could come to appeal to the Bush administration much more than a precipitate withdrawal with all the potential for chaos that that might bring. It might also be the option that would be more satisfactory to states in Western Europe and to the Iraqi government itself. There are, though, four problems. One is that there is an intrinsic opposition to the United Nations within the Bush administration that would make this a very hard policy to accept, and a second is that it would not ensure US control over the security of Iraqi oil reserves. Thirdly, there would be a deep reluctance on the part of the UN to become involved at this depth, even if troops from other Islamic countries were prepared to be involved. Finally, any kind of US withdrawal, even if carefully planned and involving the UN, would be seen across much of the region and certainly within the al-Qaeda movement, as a defeat for the USA. It would be almost as big a foreign policy reversal for Washington as precipitate withdrawal.

The final possibility is that the current insurgency lasts indefinitely, becoming something of a stalemate between weak Iraqi security forces that cannot maintain the security of the state on their own, even when backed by the US military presence, and insurgents who cannot develop sufficient strength to threaten the very survival of the Iraqi government or cause an American withdrawal. Such a situation could last for several years but might ultimately lead to some kind of compromise in which a majority of the supporters of the insurgency were brought into the political process sufficiently to undermine the insurgency itself. While this is certainly possible, it would involve some years of war, with the huge human costs that this would involve, and even such an eventual compromise is by no means certain.

The Wider War

While most analysis of the Iraq war concentrates on the insurgency as a domestic matter, it also has to be seen in its wider context. In parallel with developments in Iraq, the spring and early summer of 2005 have seen a marked increase in the activity of Taliban and other paramilitaries in Afghanistan, with increasing US concern over the failure of the Pakistani government to rein in radical Islamic elements or to suppress paramilitary activities in the districts close to the Afghan border.

The al-Qaeda movement has remained active elsewhere, not least with the attacks in Indonesia and Egypt towards the end of 2004. There was less activity outside of the Middle East and South West Asia in the first half of 2005, but a series of four bomb attacks, three of them closely coordinated, on the London transport system on 7 July brought that period to an end. Although not on the scale of the Madrid bombings in March

2004, the London attacks were devastating in their human cost, as well as demonstrating that the al-Qaeda movement and its loose affiliates retained an ability to operate in Western Europe.

In relation to Iraq and the wider war on terror, over the past two years that country has become a magnet for radical Islamic paramilitaries, giving a substantial boost for recruitment into movements such as al-Qaeda and providing a basis for a region-wide growth in anti-Americanism. Even if the insurgency within Iraq does eventually diminish, with some degree of political compromise achieved, a core aspect of US policy will still be the maintenance of permanent bases in the context of that essential feature of US policy in the Middle East, ensuring the security of Gulf oil reserves.

The issue of oil geopolitics remains fundamental to both the ongoing war in Iraq and the wider global 'war on terror', yet it remains largely ignored by most analysts in spite of the remarkable concentration of oil reserves in Iraq and surrounding states.[13] The main oil producers of the Persian Gulf – Saudi Arabia, Iraq, Iran, Kuwait and the United Arab Emirates – together have about sixty-five per cent of all the world's known oil reserves, with most of it cheap to extract and of relatively high quality. This compares with barely three per cent for the continental USA, including Alaska, and a broadly similar figure for China and also for the whole of Europe.

Furthermore, all the major industrial and industrialising regions of the world are increasingly dependent on Gulf oil as non-Gulf reserves decrease more quickly. This includes the USA, Western Europe, China, Japan and India. It does much to explain the substantial US security interest in the Gulf region, especially since the oil price rises of 1973,[14] and the development of the Joint Report Deployment Task Force and its elevation to a unified military command, Central Command (CENTCOM) in the 1990s.[15] The USA imported around ten per cent of its oil requirements in 1970, but this has risen to fifty-eight per cent in 2005. China regards the Persian Gulf as being a region of core strategic importance and, among other responses, has concluded very substantial agreements with Iran for the long-term supply of oil and natural gas.

Iran itself remains a major issue for the US security posture in the region, with neoconservative elements in Washington still insistent on the need to prevent Iran developing a civil nuclear infrastructure, let alone any kind of nuclear weapons programme. While such an outlook may be constrained by problems in Iraq, opposition from European allies and the skill of Iranian diplomats in systematic prevarication, there remains the attitude of Israel, given that it has acquired long-range strike aircraft and an enhanced aerial refuelling capability from the USA. Furthermore, while it is the nuclear issue that is dominant in US attitudes towards Iran, secondary to this is the recognition of Iran's own energy reserves, especially in its position as being second only to Russia in the size of its natural gas reserves.

The importance of Gulf energy resources links directly with the evolution of the al-Qaeda movement and its affiliates, since the perception of foreign interference in the Islamic Middle East is fundamental to the outlook of such groups. Although the al-Qaeda movement has a particular interest in the Israeli-Palestinian confrontation, and in specific regional areas of conflict such as southern Thailand, at the heart of its outlook is opposition to the House of Saud, as the illegitimate Keeper of the Two Holy Places, a more general opposition to the elitist and West-leaning regimes of much of the Arab Middle East, and a long-term desire to reconceptualise the historic idea of an Islamic caliphate (see Chapter 7). There is thus a fundamental conflict between a US insistence on maintaining Gulf security as a core feature of its global security policy, and a deep-seated antagonism to such a policy that is being made worse by the US occupation of Baghdad, the historic seat of the most notable Islamic caliphate.

At root, this perception of a neo-Christian/Zionist process of controlling Arab oil and preventing the development of true Islamic governance is an extraordinarily powerful mindset that lies at the heart of many of the problems the USA is facing. Moreover, it is not just an opposition stemming from elements within one of the three 'Religions of the Book', Judaism, Christianity and Islam; it is an opposition that is mirrored in aspects of both of the other two religions. Radical Zionists in Israel retain their belief in the core requirement for a Greater Israel, seeking the relocation of Palestinians even more vigorously as the size of the Palestinian population in Israel and the occupied territories begins to approach that of Jewish Israel.

Perhaps more significant in the current context is the extent to which Christian radicals have a particular and unusual power base within US domestic politics (see Chapter 10). If the geopolitics of oil is one factor that is too often ignored in the analysis of the global war on terror, then the rise to political significance of Christian Zionism in the USA is another. Concern with the 'end times' is a fundamental aspect of Pentecostals and Fundamentalists on the religious right, with such groups making up many tens of millions of voters. Moreover this orientation is part of greater influence that religion has gained within US governance in the past five years. It is more potent than at any time since 'Imperial America' in the early years of the twentieth century, or possibly even going back to the millennial influences in pre-revolutionary colonial America.[16]

Although the USA has many serious problems in the Middle East, especially in Iraq, the unlikely combination of the huge importance of Gulf oil reserves and the influence of religious fundamentalists within the Bush administration means that it will be formidably difficult to envisage a fundamental change in policy in the near future. Given that the al-Qaeda movement and its affiliates are seeking to achieve their aims over a period of decades rather than years, the probability is that, short of major political changes in the USA, the Iraq war might well be measured over a similar time span.

Notes

Introduction

1. Frank Barnaby, *The New Terrorism: A 21ˢᵗ Century Biological, Chemical and Nuclear Threat*, Oxford Research Group report, December 2001.

2. Paul Rogers and Scilla Elworthy, *The United States, Europe and the Majority World after 11 September*, Oxford Research Group briefing paper, October 2001.

3. Paul Rogers, *Iraq: Consequences of a War*, Oxford Research Group briefing paper, October 2002.

4. Philip H. Gordon, Martin Indyk, Michael E. O'Hanlon, 'Getting Serious About Iraq', *Survival*, Vol. 42, No. 3, Autumn 2002.

5. Available at www.oxfordresearchgroup.org.uk.

6. Paul Rogers, *Iraq and the War on Terror: Oxford Research Group International Security Report 2004*, Oxford Research Group, July 2004.

Chapter 1. Regime Termination and the Evolving War

1. This chapter provides a context for the analysis of the second year of the Iraq war, summarising the main conclusions of the earlier report, *Iraq and the War on Terror* (2004).

2. The source for this table is www.icasualties.org/oif/, the website for Iraq Coalition Casualty Count, an independent organisation providing detailed data on US military casualties in Iraq.

3. The first substantive report of the development of permanent bases in Iraq was in the *New York Times* in April 2003; see: Paul Rogers, 'Permanent Occupation?', *Open Democracy*, 24 April 2003, available at www.opendemocracy.net.

4. In the period from the start of the Iraq war in March 2003 through to April 2004, there were numerous attacks. They included multiple bombings of western targets in Casablanca in May 2003, killing thirty-nine people and injuring sixty, and multiple bombings in the Saudi capital, Riyadh, the same month, that killed twenty-nine people and injured 200. In August 2003, the Marriott Hotel in the Indonesian capital, Djakarta, was bombed, killing thirteen and injuring 149 and, in November, two synagogues in Istanbul were bombed, killing twenty-four people and injuring 255, followed shortly by the bombing of the UK consulate and the HSBC bank in the same city, killing twenty-seven and injuring 400. In March 2004, the multiple bombing of commuter trains in Madrid killed 200 people and injured over 1,000.

Chapter 2. Problems on Two Fronts: May 2004

1. Kerry's caution was surprising in the face of growing concerns among senior military officers over the course of the occupation. The concern was not that they could not control the insurgency but that they were failing to win the support of Iraqis; see Thomas E. Ricks, 'Dissension Grows in Senior Ranks on War Strategy', *Washington Post*, 9 May 2004. Furthermore, it was now becoming accepted that the USA would have to keep substantial numbers of troops in Iraq, perhaps as many as 135,000 and certainly more than earlier plans to shrink troops numbers to between 105,000 and 115,000; see 'U.S. to Keep High Force Levels in Iraq Indefinitely', *Agence France-Presse*, 3 May 2004.

2. The revolt of Shi'ite paramilitaries had developed in April, principally in the cities of Kufa and Najaf but also in the Sadr City district of Baghdad. The conflict broke out on 3 April and involved the militias of a cleric, Moqtada al-Sadr, fighting primarily against US forces. On the first day alone, eight US soldiers were killed and over thirty wounded, and at least twenty Iraqi demonstrators were killed; see Karl Vick and Saad Sarhan, 'Eight U.S. Troops Killed in Shiite Uprising', *Washington Post*, 5 April 2004. During the course of the fighting, there were frequent indications that the US forces intended to detain Moqtada al-Sadr but an agreement had been reached by the end of the month, involving mutual US and militia withdrawals from Najaf; see Justin Hugler, 'U.S. Retreats after Failing to Capture Militia Chief', *The Independent*, 28 May 2004.

3. In the intense fighting in April 2004, 135 US troops were killed, but the

losses in May were also high, with eighty killed. Large numbers of troops were also being injured: in the four-week period from 4 to 31 May 2004, over 750 US personnel were injured, the majority of them seriously. See Iraq Coalition Casualty Count, www.icasualties.org/.

4. Although there was increasing concern over economic targeting by insurgents, other forms of insurgency continued, including the use of suicide bombs. In one of the most high-profile attacks, the president of the Iraqi Governing Council was assassinated on 17 May by a suicide bomber who also killed nine other people. The president, Izzedine Salim, was the leader of the influential Shi'ite group the Dawa Party. His killing added to a mood of despair among many Iraqis at the failure of the occupying forces to ensure stability. See Sewell Chan and Scott Wilson, 'Violence Leaves Iraqis in Despair', *Washington Post*, 19 May 2004.

5. The existing level of attacks was already causing serious problems for the USA, and one response was to use Israeli counter-insurgency experience more widely, including the provision of improved armour for US Army vehicles in the face of widespread insurgent use of rocket-propelled grenades. See Barbara Opall-Rome, 'U.S. Rushes to Deploy Israel's Hefty Armor Kits', *Defense News*, 17 May 2004.

6. On 21 April, a suicide bomber had killed two senior police officers and three other people in an attack on government building in Riyadh, and the month of May was marked by four attacks: 1 May – the offices of the Houston-based ABB Lummus Global Inc in the port of Yanbu were attacked, killing six western employees and a Saudi; 20 May – Saudi security forces killed four suspects in an exchange of fire near Buraida; 22 May – a German man was shot dead in a Riyadh street; 29 May – four foreigners and two Saudis were killed in an attack on an oil compound in Khobar. See 'Gunmen "Killed 22" in Saudi City', BBC News, 30 May 2004.

Chapter 3. Transfer of Power or Client Regime? June 2004

1. Although tensions eased markedly in the city of Najaf, violence continued elsewhere. Five people were killed in a Shi'a area of Baghdad on 6 June in an attack on civilian contractors, and two US soldiers were killed by a roadside bomb, also in a Shi'a area. See Edward Cody, 'Clash with Shiites Shifts to Baghdad; Seven Killed', *Washington Post*, 6 June 2004.

2. Daniel Williams, 'Despite Agreement, Insurgents Rule Fallujah', *Washington Post*, 7 June 2004.

3. There was relatively little information in the public domain concerning these controls until right at the end of June, just before the handover to Mr Alawi; see Rajiv Chandrasekaran and Walter Pincus, 'U.S. Edicts Curb Power of Iraq's Leadership', *Washington Post*, 27 June 2004.

4. The violence across much of Iraq continued throughout June, including assassinations of government ministers and officials. On 12 June, a Deputy Foreign Minister, Bassam Kuba, was shot dead. He was regarded as the Ministry's most senior career diplomat and was an expert on legal issues; see Aljazeera.net, 12 June 2004. Four days later, on 16 June, the head of security for the oil industry in northern Iraq was attacked and killed outside his home. Ghazi al-Talibana was reported to be related to one of the most senior Kurdish politicians in Iraq, Jalal Talabani, head of the Patriotic Union of Kurdistan; see 'Iraqi Oil Official Is Gunned Down', BBC News, 16 June 2004.

5. Although there was a hope that the political transition in Iraq and the development of Iraqi security forces would ease pressures on US forces, the US Army was reported to be preparing the first involuntary call-up of troops from the Individual Ready Reserve (IRR) in over a decade, with at least 5,600 people called up. Furthermore, the Army had started pre-screening the entire IRR force of 117,400 troops to determine eligibility for deployment; see Lisa Burgess, 'Army Prepares to Activate At Least 5,600 Troops from Individual Ready Reserves', *Stars and Stripes*, European Edition, 30 June 2004. There were also further links with the Israeli armed forces to ensure that their experience in seeking to control the al-Aqsa *intifada* could be applied in Iraq: 'For the second time in six months, senior brass from the U.S. Army's Training and Doctrine Command (TRADOC) met with Israeli military and industry leaders to flesh out tactical and technological solutions for anti-terror, urban operations.' Barbara Opal-Rome, 'Seeking Urban Ops Answers in Israel', *Defense News*, 14 June 2004.

6. During June, five members of staff of the French MSF medical charity were killed in one incident and, in another, eleven Chinese road contractors were killed. In a move aimed at disrupting preparations for the forthcoming election, due in September, a series of attacks killed five election officials and sixteen people who had registered to vote; see *Monthly Review, June 2004*, British Agencies Afghanistan Group, London, July 2004. At the end of May, four US soldiers were killed in an incident in the southern province

of Zabul. It was reported that over 700 people had died in attacks in Afghanistan in the previous ten months. See Aljazeera.net, 5 June 2004.

7. What became evident during June was that al-Qaeda-linked paramilitaries were putting more of their resources into targeting western expatriates, with attacks stretching across the country. In being able to do so, they also demonstrated a degree of support within Saudi society. According to a retired Saudi Army major general, Enwar Eshkie, director of the Jeddah-based Centre for Strategic and Legal Studies, 'The terrorists do enjoy a good level of support within sections of the Saudi society... otherwise, they would not have been able to hide and move around in the country undetected.' Riad Kahwaji, 'Terrorists Switch Tactics', *Defense News*, 14 June 2004.

Chapter 4. Iran Comes into the Frame: July 2004

1. US forces staged repeated air strikes on the city of Fallujah. One such attack, on 17 July, was the sixth on the city in a month and killed fourteen people. The new prime minister, Mr Alawi, was reported to have approved the raids; see Danica Kirka, 'U.S. Airstrike in Fallujah Kills 14', *Associated Press*, 18 July 2004.

2. On taking office, the Alawi administration immediately introduced a law giving the administration 'broad powers of martial rule in troubled areas, including direct command of army, police and intelligence units'; see Rajiv Chandrasekaran and Walter Pincus, 'Iraq Approves Law Allowing Martial Rule', *Washington Post*, 7 July 2004.

3. See Iraq Coalition Casualty Count, www.icasualties.org.

4. Among the many attacks during July, ten people were killed and forty wounded near the Green Zone in Baghdad on 14 July, and the Governor of Mosul was killed in an ambush on the same day. The following day, ten people were killed in an attack on a police station in Haditha; two days later, four bodyguards of the Iraqi Justice Minister were killed in an attempted assassination of the Minister; and, two days after that, another police station, in the Seidiyeh district south-west of Baghdad was attacked with a car bomb, killing five and injuring more than thirty. See 'Iraq's New Battle of Wills', BBC News, 19 July 2004. The same day, a senior official at the Ministry of Defence was shot dead near his home in Baghdad and, on 19 June, the interim governor of Basra Province was assassinated; Bloomberg News, 20 July 2004. At the end of July, one month after the appointment of

the Alawi administration, a large car bomb killed sixty-eight people and injured many more in an attack on a police station at Baquba, north-east of Baghdad; see 'Scores Killed in Iraq Bomb Attack', BBC News, 28 July 2004.

5.   Pepe Escobar 'The Islamic Emirate of Fallujah', *Asia Times*, 15 July 2004.

6.   For example, eleven Afghans, including a former police chief, were killed in the southern province of Helmand on 21 July following an attack the previous day in Uruzgan Province where US and Afghan government forces came under attack in an incident that left six people dead. See Aljazeera.net, 22 July 2004.

7.   'Focus: Next Stop Iran', *The Times Online*, 25 July 2004.

Chapter 5. A Change of Direction? August 2004

1.   As had been expected, one aspect of the insurgency was the use of economic targeting, especially against oil facilities, with this seriously hindering efforts at reconstruction. For example, an attack on a cluster of around twenty oil pipelines near Basra on 25 August cut exports by half and followed an arson attack against the South Oil Company's headquarters the previous week. See 'Iraq Oil Exports Cut in Half After Attack', *Associated Press*, 26 August 2004.

2.   Although most of the international focus on the conflict in Iraq during August was on the fighting in the city of Najaf, there was also substantial conflict elsewhere. In the city of Samarra, the US forces mounted Operation 'Cajun Mousetrap III' against insurgents. On the night of 14–15 August, thirteen Iraqis were killed and eighty-four wounded in one period of fighting, and at least fifty more Iraqis were killed in US bombing raids. See 'Many Killed in US Bombing of Samarra', Aljazeera.net, 14 August 2004. Air strikes on the city of Fallujah also continued, including one on 14 August that killed eight and injured ten. See 'US Air Raid on Falluja Kills Women, Children', Aljazeera.net, 14 August 2004.

3.   Najaf was one of the cities that initially welcomed US forces when the regime of Saddam Hussein was terminated in April 2003. In the wake of the fighting in the city during August 2004, the mood had changed substantially towards outright opposition to what was now seen as foreign occupation. See Tim Ripley, 'Shia Backlash Wrecks U.S. Strategy', *The Scotsman*, 15 August 2004.

4.   The conflict in Najaf left the holy city severely damaged. Weapons used by US forces included 25mm chain guns on Bradley Fighting Vehicles,

120mm guns on tanks, 155mm howitzers, Apache helicopter gunships and fixed-wing strike aircraft. Although efforts were made to avoid damage to the Imam Ali shrine, buildings around it were heavily damaged as were many other mosques and school buildings that had been used as bases by insurgents. See Karl Vick, 'Iraq Holy City Left Broken by Urban Warfare', *Washington Post*, 27 August 2004.

5.   Information on this potentially significant development came from one of the few news organisations operating widely across Iraq, the London-based Institute for War and Peace Reporting. See, in particular, Aqil Jabar, 'Mahdi Army Draws Supporters', *Iraq Crisis Report No 78*, IWPR, 11 August 2004. See also Zainab Naji, 'Combat Training, Courtesy of Fallujah', *Iraq Crisis Report No 80*, IWPR, 24 August 2004.

6.   The Iraq Body Count group, based in the UK, publishes its civilian casualty estimates in substantial detail and uses a very conservative methodology, normally requiring reliable press reports before particular casualty levels are accepted as being plausible. While this may mean that estimates of casualties are low, it also involves a high degree of reliability for the actual figures published. See www.iraqbodycount.net.

7.   For details see www.fightingterror.org/. The re-launch for the Committee was described by the new Joint Chairs, Senators Joe Lieberman and Jon Kyl, in an article, 'The Present Danger', *Washington Post*, 20 July, 2004. For an analysis of the origins and development of the CPD and of its new role, see Jim Lobe, 'They're Back: Neocons Revive the Committee on the Present Danger, This Time Against Terrorism', *Foreign Policy in Focus*, Interhemispheric Resource Centre, Washington, July 2004, www.fpif.org/.

Chapter 6. Iraq and a Wider War: September 2004

1.   By early September, the toll of US military deaths had passed 1,000. In addition, August had been a particularly bad month for injuries, with US forces experiencing about 1,100 injured, primarily because of the intense fighting in Fallujah. See Karl Vick, 'U.S. Troops in Iraq See Highest Injury Toll Yet', *Washington Post*, 5 September 2004. The Iraqi civilian death toll was very much higher. External organisations such as Iraq Body Count put the total civilian casualties from the start of the war at between 11,800 and 13,800, and Amnesty International put the figure for the first year at 10,000. For a relatively short period during 2004, the Iraqi Ministry of Health published its own figures that showed, for example, that, between 5 April

and 31 August 2004, 2,956 civilians were killed 'as a result of a military act', including 125 children. See Bassem Mroue, 'Thousands of Iraqis Killed', *Associated Press*, 8 September 2004.

2. In addition, attacks continued on economic targets – the largest single pipeline attack happened on 2 September when a forty-inch pipe was blown up, producing a very large fire that engulfed much of the near-by city of Kirkuk in black smoke. See 'Massive Blast Disrupts Iraqi Oil Exports', Aljazeera.net, 2 September 2004.

3. Around the middle of 2004, NATO had provided approximately 6,500 troops for ISAF and managed to obtain 1,500 more troops for the period around the October elections. Its wider role was, in part, to train an effective national army of around 70,000 by 2009, prior to leaving the country, but only 15,000 had been trained in the three years following the termination of the Taliban regime. See Craig S. Smith, 'NATO Runs Short of Troops to Expand Afghan Peacekeeping', *New York Times*, 18 September 2004.

4. 'The Struggle for Order', *The Economist*, 25 September 2004.

5. Some US military actions were particularly damaging in terms of relations with Iraqi communities. In one incident in Baghdad on 13 September, for example, a US military helicopter fired into a crowd surrounding a burning US Army armoured vehicle, killing thirteen people including a journalist with the al-Arabiya satellite news channel. The US military later said it was attempting to scatter looters but al-Arabiya TV sources disputed this. See Jackie Spinner, 'At Least 80 Civilians Die in Iraqi Violence', *Washington Post*, 13 September 2004.

Chapter 7. Iraq, al-Qaeda and a Renewed Caliphate: October 2004

1. In one of the worst incidents, forty-nine recently trained Iraqi National Guard recruits were murdered while on their way to a period of leave pending their initial deployments; see Karl Vick, 'Insurgents Massacre 49 Iraqi Recruits', *Washington Post*, 25 October 2004.

2. The main assault on Samarra started on 30 September and was one of the largest US operations mounted in Iraq since regime termination in April the previous year. It involved 3,000 US troops supported by 2,000 soldiers, police and national guard. See Karl Vick, 'Troops Battle to Control Samarra', *Washington Post*, 2 October 2004. While initially successful, in that many key sites were occupied, insurgents returned later in the month after most US forces had moved on to other operations.

3. Two different indicators of the strain on US forces were reported at the time. The Defense Science Board, a group of external advisers to the Pentagon, reported that the US military did not have sufficient personnel to meet probable commitments in the coming years. Its recommendations included adding a substantial number of troops while cutting back on peacekeeping operations. See Mark Mazzetti, 'U.S. Military is Stretched Too Thin, Defense Board Warns', *Los Angeles Times*, 30 September 2004. Some indication of the health costs of the war was shown by figures released from the Department of Veterans Affairs, reporting that 26,633 veterans of operations in Iraq and Afghanistan had filed benefits claims for what was described as 'service-connected disabilities' for the period to the end of April 2004. See Josh White, 'Influx of Wounded Strains VA', *Washington Post*, 3 October 2004. More generally, the Bush administration was requesting a substantial increase in funding for the war and the continuing conflict in Afghanistan. $70 billion was likely to be sought, bringing the total cost of the two conflicts from March 2003 to $225 billion. See Jonathan Weisman and Thomas E. Ricks, 'Increase in War Funding Sought', *Washington Post*, 26 October 2004.

4. An assault on Fallujah, in particular, was regarded as essential in order to limit the likely impact of the insurgency on the elections planned for January. Even though this was regarded as an urgent requirement, there were reports that the Bush administration had decided to hold back the operation until after the US presidential election in early November, because of the possible effect on the election of a major military operation in Iraq. See Mark Mazzetti, 'Major Assaults on Hold Until After U.S. Vote', *Los Angeles Times*, 11 October 2004.

5. See www.iraqbodycount.net.

6. Les Roberts, Riyadh Lafta, Richard Garfield, Jamal Khudhairi, Gilbert Burnham, 'Mortality before and after the 2003 Invasion of Iraq: Cluster Sample Survey', *The Lancet*, published online 29 October 2004, www.thelancet.com.

7. A full transcript of bin Laden's speech is at Aljazeera.net, 30 October 2004.

8. Taken from the BBC translation.

9. The concern over the effect of the Iraq war went further than its impact on the al-Qaeda movement. The London-based International Institute for Strategic Studies reported that the Iraq occupation was hampering the US ability to handle other threats. Speaking at the launch of the Institute's

annual *Military Balance*, the director, John Chipman, commented 'Over the past year, the nuclear proliferation threat posed by North Korea and Iran has worsened, as both countries exploited America's growing troubles in Iraq.' See Antony La Guardia, 'Iraq Hampering US ability to deal with "axis of evil"', *Daily Telegraph*, 20 October 2004. In relation specifically to Iraq, there was particular concern in Saudi Arabia that the Iraq occupation was aiding the growth in support for paramilitary groups within the Kingdom. See Joe Brinkley, 'Saudis Blame U.S. and its Role in Iraq for Rise of Terror', *New York Times*, 14 October 2004. In addition, there had earlier been evidence that Saudi paramilitary elements were travelling to Iraq and using it as an environment for combat training before returning to Saudi Arabia. See Craig Whitlock, 'Saudis Facing Return of Radicals', *Washington Post*, 11 July 2004.

10.   Although with only tenuous links to the al-Qaeda movement, the separatist movement in southern Thailand experienced an attack by Thai security forces that had a substantial impact in many Islamic communities beyond Thailand, even if little reported in the western media. Following unrest in late October and a riot by separatists in Takbai district, 1,300 people were arrested. One group was transported to an army camp for detention and seventy-eight of them died of suffocation during the journey. See 'Thai Muslims suffocated to death in custody', Aljazeera.net, 26 October 2004. The following week, a Buddhist leader was murdered, apparently in a response to the incident. See 'Thai elder killed "in revenge"' BBC News, 11 November 2004.

11.   This is not to diminish the long-term significance of the continuing insecurity in Afghanistan. According to a Canadian army general, Andrew Leslie, who had been a deputy commander of the International Security Assistance Force in 2003, international forces should expect to stay in Afghanistan for ten to twenty years. See Doug Struck, 'Canadian Sees a Long Haul in Afghanistan', *Washington Post*, 16 October 2004. This rather pessimistic assessment was even made in the light of the reasonably peaceful election that had brought Hamid Karzai to the Presidency on 9 October 2004.

Chapter 8. Fallujah and its Aftermath: November 2004

1.   As the assault on Fallujah began to develop, there was an upsurge in bombings elsewhere in Iraq, with fifty-two people killed in two attacks

in a single day; see Jackie Spinner, '52 Killed in Spate of Attacks in Iraq', *Washington Post*, 7 November 2004. In addition, the most substantial attack on Iraq's oil facilities since the termination of the Saddam Hussein regime was mounted on 2 November, with the coordinated targeting of three oil pipelines in northern Iraq; see 'Massive attack halts Iraq oil flow', Aljazeera. net, 2 November 2004.

2. Eleven people were killed and 161 were injured in the bomb attack on the Australian Embassy in Djakarta, Indonesia, and twenty-seven people were killed and 122 injured in attacks on the Taba Hilton and a camp site at Nueiba in Sinai, Egypt, directed at Israeli tourists.

3. Mackubin Thomas Owens, 'Two, Three, Many Fallujas', *Weekly Standard*, 6 December 2004.

4. In other parts of Iraq there were numerous attacks on police stations and other government facilities, with US forces using air strikes in response. See Edward Wong and James Glanz, 'Iraqi Insurgents Roil Sunni Triangle with Counterattack', *New York Times*, 15 November 2004.

5. 'US launches major Mosul assault', BBC News, 16 November 2004. Later in the month, further military operations had to be mounted in towns and cities south of Baghdad, with 5,000 US, British and Iraqi troops involved in a series of actions; see Tini Tran, 'Mass Offensive Launched South of Baghdad', Associated Press, 23 November 2004.

6. There were some exceptions to this; see, for example, Michael Schwartz, 'US battle plans begin to unravel', *Asia Times*, 19 November 2004. There was also concern that the assault on Fallujah, with all the firepower involved, would make it more difficult to gain support from the wider Sunni community in Iraq; see Edward Wong, 'Breaking a City in Order to Fix It', *New York Times*, 14 November 2004.

7. There were indications that there was already a degree of pessimism within the US military over the effect of the apparently successful Fallujah assault. According to one report, 'Marine intelligence officials have issued a report warning that any significant withdrawal of troops from the Iraqi city of Fallujah would strengthen the insurgency. The assessment, distributed to senior Marine and Army officers in Iraq, also said that despite the heavy fighting with coalition forces, the insurgents would continue to increase in number, carrying out attacks and fomenting unrest in the area.' See 'U.S. Intelligence Issues Pessimistic Report on Fallujah Offensive', *Agence France Presse*, 18 November 2004.

8.   In this context, one of the significant features of the Fallujah assault was that very few of the insurgents operating in Fallujah were from other countries. Of the 1,500 men aged between fifteen and fifty-five who were detained during the assault, only fifteen were confirmed as foreign – further evidence that the insurgency was overwhelmingly indigenous. See John Hendren, 'Few Foreigners Among Insurgents', *Los Angeles Times*, 16 November 2004.

Chapter 9. Towards a Third Year of War: December 2004

1.   There were substantial attacks throughout December, with particularly violent periods near the beginning and the end of the month. Twenty-six people were killed and many more injured in attacks on a Shi'a mosque and a police station in Baghdad on 3 December and, two days later, nearly forty people were killed, mainly in attacks in Mosul and Baghdad. See 'Baghdad Hit by Two Major Attacks', BBC News, 3 December 2004; 'Car Bombings, Other Attacks Kill nearly 40 in Iraq', *Agence France Presse*, 5 December 2004. Towards the end of the month, there were major attacks on police units in several cities and towns. On 28 December, twenty-five police were killed in a series of attacks in Baghdad and Baquba and near Tikrit and, on the following day, twenty-eight police were killed in a single incident in Baghdad. See 'Many Police Killed in Baghdad Blast', Aljazeera. net, 29 December 2004.

2.   On 27 October, the Red Cross headquarters and three police stations in Baghdad were bombed in a coordinated attack that killed 35 people and injured 230.

3.   See Thomas E Ricks, 'Precision of Base Attack Worries Military Experts', *Washington Post*, 22 December 2004.

4.   In one of the more remarkable indicators of the degree of insecurity, the US Embassy within the heavily protected Green Zone in the centre of Baghdad stopped its employees using the ten-mile road linking the city centre with the international airport. Even though the road was guarded by 1,000 members of the Army's 1st Cavalry Division and passengers were normally transported in a heavily armoured vehicle accompanied by armoured escorts, it was deemed insufficiently safe for diplomats who would henceforth use helicopters. See Bradley Graham, 'U.S. Embassy Bans Use of Airport Road', *Washington Post*, 3 December 2004.

5.   The role of Syria was highlighted both by military intelligence sources

(Thomas E Ricks, 'Rebels Aided By Allies in Syria, U.S. Says', *Washington Post*, 8 December 2004) and particularly by commentators on the neoconservative wing of the Republican Party (William Kristol, 'Getting Serious About Syria', *Weekly Standard*, 20 December 2004).

6. This was in spite of renewed controversy over the treatment of detainees in Iraq, following the publication of photographs showing prisoner abuse by Navy SEAL special forces, photographs widely distributed in the media across the Middle East. See 'US investigating new prisoner abuse photos', Aljazeera.net, 4 December 2004.

Chapter 10. Elections and Their Consequences: January 2005

1. As President Bush himself put it: 'We had an accountability moment, and that's called the 2004 elections. The American people listened to different assessments made about what was taking place in Iraq, and they looked at the two candidates, and chose me.' See Jim VandeHei and Michael A Fletcher, 'Bush Says Election Ratified Iraq Policy', *Washington Post*, 16 January 2005.

2. A succinct analysis of the development of Christian Zionism by Donald Wagner is available at www.informationclearinghouse.info/article4959. htm. See also Steven Sizer, 'Christian Zionism: Road Map to Armageddon', www.Christchurch-virginiawater.co.uk/articles/ivp.html.

3. The second half of 2004 was actually the worst six-month period for US casualties since the war began, with over 500 soldiers killed; see 'Final Six Months Deadliest Ever for US Forces in Iraq', *Agence France-Presse*, 1 January 2005. One effect of the insurgency was to cause a re-evaluation of the defence budget, with some spending intended for new advanced technology projects curbed in favour of more spending on troops and routine equipment for the Army; see Jonathan Weisman and Renae Merle, 'Pentagon Scales back Arms Plans', *Washington Post*, 5 January 2005.

4. One of the features of the continuing insurgency in Iraq was seen to be that it was replacing Afghanistan as a training ground for paramilitary elements from elsewhere, even though the vast majority of the insurgents were Iraqis. According to David B. Low, the CIA's national intelligence officer for transnational skills, Iraq provides them with 'a training ground, a recruitment ground, the opportunity for enhancing technical skills'; see Dana Priest, 'Iraq New Terror Breeding Ground', *Washington Post*, 14 January 2005.

5.   Bradley Graham, 'Army Plans to Keep Iraq Troop Level Through '06', *Washington Post*, 25 January 2005.

6.   Such a robust policy was in the context of an argument put by some analysts that the administration had also consolidated its control over the military and intelligence communities to an extent unmatched since the Second World War. See, for example: Seymour M Hersh, 'The Coming Wars: What the Pentagon Can Now Do in Secret', *New Yorker*, 24 January 2005.

Chapter 11. Limitations of Power: February 2005

1.   Robin Wright, 'Iraq Winners Allied With Iran Are the Opposite of U.S. Vision', *Washington Post*, 14 February 2005.

2.   An additional problem for US forces was maintaining order in the large detention centres established in Iraq. The largest, Camp Bucca, is near the Kuwait border and commonly houses over 5,000 detainees. Although not widely reported until three weeks after the event, four detainees were killed and six injured when US Army guards used live ammunition to quell a riot affecting five of the eight compounds, non-lethal methods having failed to control the situation. See Bradley Graham, 'Prison Uprising in Iraq Exposes New Risk for U.S.', *Washington Post*, 21 February 2005.

3.   There had been an expectation that the level of security maintained by US and Iraqi forces immediately prior to the election would limit insurgent activity. In fact, the lull in violence was short-lived, with two attacks on police units, in Mosul and Baquba on 7 February, killing twenty-seven people and wounding many more. See 'Dozens killed in multiple Iraq blasts', Aljazeera.net, 7 February 2005.

4.   Dan Murphy, 'Iraq's neighbourhood councils are vanishing', *Christian Science Monitor*, 25 February 2005.

5.   See James Glanz, 'Insurgents attacking Baghdad's lifelines', *New York Times*, 22 February 2005.

6.   In addition to the ongoing insurgency in Iraq, Kuwait was also experiencing incidents of radical paramilitary activity; see Mary Ann Tetreault, 'Terrorist Violence in Kuwait', *Foreign Policy in Focus*, 23 February 2005, www.fpif. org.

7.   One action, falling short of a military confrontation, was the proposal to increase aid to Iran's opposition groups, and a new $3 million fund was established for this purpose; see Sonni Efron and Mark Mazzetti, 'Officials at

State have Money in Hand but Are still Weighing How Best to Effect Change', *Los Angeles Times*, 4 March 2005.

8. One part of the US actions in relation to Iran was the use of pilotless drones flying over the country. While the primary purpose was said to be the gathering of information on a possible nuclear weapons programme, a secondary function was detecting weaknesses in the Iranian air defence system. See Dafna Linzer, 'U.S. Uses Drones to Probe Iran for Arms', *Washington Post*, 13 February 2005.

Chapter 12. The Bush Administration, Insurgencies and Iran: March 2005

1. There were also instances of violence against expatriates in Kabul. A British rural development adviser, Steven MacQueen, was shot dead in Kabul on 8 March, the seventh expatriate to be killed in Kabul in the past year. See N.C. Aizenman, 'British Man Shot and Killed in Kabul', *Washington Post*, 8 March 2005.

2. 'Afghanistan Now Nearly a "Narcotics State"', *Associated Press*, 4 March 2005. At the same time, UN sources indicated that there might be a fall in opium poppy production in 2005, partly because of increased action by the Karzai administration, but also due to low yields in the previous season and a fall in prices paid to growers. The fall in prices might have been due to the major increase in the previous year's production. There were also suggestions from UN sources that any fall in poppy cultivation might not be sustained. See *Afghanistan: Monthly Review, March 2005*, British Agencies Afghanistan Group, London, April 2005.

3. Tom Barry, 'Bolton's Baggage', *International Relations Centre*, 11 March 2005, www.irc-online.org.

4. A further complication came from the pressure that appeared to be coming from Israel for the USA to take pre-emptive action against Iran; see Rowan Scarborough, 'Israel pushes U.S. on Iran nuke solution', *Washington Times*, 21 February 2005.

Chapter 13. The Iraq Impasse: April 2005

1. A difficult issue for the United States was that the coalition of states committing troops to Iraq was become more limited in number. The Netherlands and Ukraine began to withdraw their forces during the early part of 2005, Poland announced in April 2005 that it would withdraw its

forces by the end of the year and Italy indicated that it wished to end its commitments in Iraq. See 'Poland confirms Iraq withdrawal', BBC News, 13 April 2005. More surprisingly, it was reported that the UK intended to reduce the size of its forces in Iraq from 9,000 to 3,500 within twelve months, partly to enable it to increase its deployments in Afghanistan. See Sean Rayment, 'Britain to Pull 5,500 Troops out of Iraq', *Sunday Telegraph*, 3 April 2005.

2.   There was a particular intensity of violence around the time of the visits of Deputy Secretary of State Robert Zoellick and Secretary of Defense Donald Rumsfeld in the middle of April; see 'Iraqi Violence Flares as US's Zoellick Visits', Reuters, 13 April 1005. During Mr Rumsfeld's visit, he argued strongly against any major purge of the security forces by the Shi'ite-majority government. The concern was that such a purge would be directed at Sunni members of the forces considered to have Ba'athist sympathies; see Ellen Knickmeyer, 'Rumsfeld Urges Iraqi Leaders Not to Purge Security Forces', *Washington Post*, 13 April 2005. This was in the context of further reports that the training of Iraqi security forces was proving deeply problematic; see Spencer Ante, 'In Iraq, Security in Name Only', *Business Week*, 18 April 2005.

3.   See Iraq Coalition Casualty Count at www.icasualties.org/oif/. In April 2005, information finally became available about casualties among UK forces in Iraq. While a record of the deaths had previously been available, details of injuries and medical evacuations were not. Since the termination of the Saddam Hussein regime in April 2003, the UK has maintained at least 9,000 troops in Iraq and, during the Armed Forces Personnel debate in the House of Commons on 20 January 2005, the Labour Member of Parliament, Tam Dalyell, asked for information on casualties. The Minister of State for the Armed Forces, Adam Ingram, replied to Mr Dalyell on 22 April with the following information: 'Between 26 February 2003 and 28 February 2005, 2,937 personnel were evacuated from Iraq for medical reasons. In Afghanistan, since 1 January 2004, 43 personnel have been evacuated for medical reasons. This includes UK service personnel and a small number of entitled civilians who have been medically evacuated through the UK aeromedical chain. Medical reasons include illness as well as injuries. It also includes both those who have been injured in action, and those who have been injured in accidents and other incidents. The medical evacuation statistics

do not allow a distinction to be drawn between these categories. In Iraq, since August 2004, we have been collecting more detailed statistics on the number of personnel wounded in action. As a result, I can tell you that, between 1 August 2004 and 28 February 2005, seventy-six personnel were wounded in action, of which forty-four were medically evacuated, and thirty-two returned to unit.' (Source, personal information from Mr Dalyell, but the letter was also placed by the Minister in the House of Commons Library) Assuming most UK troops are on an approximately six month rotation and that a proportion will have served more than one term in Iraq, it is probable that around 30,000 UK service personnel have served in the country since the start of the war, suggesting that one in ten has been evacuated for medical reasons. It is also interesting to note that the Minister gives figures for evacuations from Iraq (not Kuwait and Iraq) starting on 26 February 2003, three weeks before the start of the war. This may point to UK special forces operating in the country before that.

4.   Iraq Body Count, www.iraqbodycount.net/.

5.   In the latter half of April, and in the run-up to the second anniversary of President Bush's 'mission accomplished' address on 1 May 2003, there were numerous attacks across Iraq. Over 100 Iraqis died in the third week of the month alone; see Ellen Knickmeyer, 'Insurgent Violence Escalates in Iraq', *Washington Post*, 24 April 2005. Four waves of attacks on 29 April killed 50 people in a single day; see Naseer Nouri and Bassam Sebti, 'String of Explosions Kill 50 in Iraq', *Washington Post*, 30 April 2005. In an unusually candid assessment of the insurgency, the Chair of the US Joint Chiefs of Staff, General Richard Myers, acknowledged that the insurgency was undiminished, with between fifty and sixty attacks occurring every day, the same as in 2004; see 'Iraqi insurgency "undiminished"', BBC News, 27 April 2005. In a UN report presented to the UN Human Rights Commission in Geneva, it had earlier been found that malnutrition rates among children under five in Iraq had more than doubled to eight per cent between March 2003 and December 2004; see 'Children "Starving" in New Iraq', BBC News, 31 March 2005. In spite of these indicators, the Bush administration remained confident of progress. In a speech at Fort Hood, Texas, on 12 April, President Bush compared the termination of the Saddam Hussein regime to the collapse of the Berlin Wall in 1989, seeing it as a democratic message being heard across the Middle East. 'As the

Iraq democracy succeeds, that success is sending a message from Beirut to Tehran that freedom can be the future of every nation,' he said. See 'Bush upbeat on Iraqi transition', BBC News, 12 April 2005.

Chapter 14. Iraq and the War on Terror: Year Two

1. www.icasualties.org/oif/.
2. www.iraqbodycount.net.
3. *Strategic Survey 2004/5*, International Institute for Strategic Studies, 2005.
4. Ibid.
5. Pepe Escobar, 'Exit Strategy: Civil War', *Asian Times*, 10 June 2005.
6. The Green Zone is the heavily guarded area of closed-off streets in central Baghdad where US occupation authorities live and work.
7. Emnad El-Din Aysha, 'September 11 and the Middle East Failure of US "Soft Power": Globalisation contra Americanisation in the "New" US Century', *International Relations*, Vol. 19, No. 2, pp. 193–210, June 2005.
8. See, for example, Bruce Hoffman, 'The Changing Face of Al Qaeda and the Global War on Terrorism', *Studies in Conflict and Terrorism*, Vol. 27, pp. 549–60, 2004. For a detailed assessment of the Iraq insurgency, see the writings of Anthony Cordesman of the Center for Strategic and International Studies, Washington, DC, e.g. Anthony H. Cordesman, *The Developing Iraqi Insurgency: Status at End-2004*, CSIS Working Draft, 22 December 2004.
9. See Chapter 13, note 5.
10. See 'Iraq "No More Safe than in 2003"', BBC News, 14 June 2005. Also quoted on Aljazeera.net, 14 June 2005.
11. See Chapter 1, note 3.
12. Martin Sieff, 'Bush, Rice Rein in Neocons on Iraq', www.spacewar.com, 15 June 2005.
13. A notable exception being Michael Klare; see his most recent book, *Blood and Oil*, Hamish Hamilton, 2004.
14. Paul Rogers (ed.), *Future Resources and World Development*, Plenum Press, 1976.
15. Explored more fully in Paul Rogers and Malcolm Dando, *A Violent Peace: Global Security After the Cold War*, Brasseys, 1992.
16. A succinct analysis of the influence of religion in US politics, both in historical context and in relation to current trends, is a paper by John Judis, 'The Chosen Nation: The Influence of Religion on U.S. Foreign Policy', *Policy Brief 37*, Carnegie Endowment for International Peace, Washington,

DC, March 2005, also available online at www.CarnegieEndowment.org).
In relation to millennialists, Judis argues that: 'For most of the last century,
many of them eschewed politics and had no view of foreign policy, except
for a strong interest in the Jewish return to Israel. Even now, when many
have entered politics primarily to combat what they see as a secular threat
to their faith, they remain wedded to a very narrow view of U.S. foreign
policy objectives focused on Israel. Much of the religious right backed the
war in Iraq not because they wanted to democratize the Middle East but
precisely because Saddam Hussein had threatened Israel, which they are
determined to protect in preparation for the end times.'

Index